Praise for *The Nonverbal Advantage*

"Given today's technology-driven communication systems, people have fewer face-to-face interactions. As a result, it is crucial to maximize their impact. Dr. Goman provides a valuable guide for doing just that by helping the reader understand how the nonverbal aspects of a conversation often say much more than the verbal ones."

— **Jon Peters**, President, The Institute for Management Studies

"*The Nonverbal Advantage* takes a fresh look at body language as an essential executive management skill. This is a must-read for anyone who is responsible for negotiating or facilitating change in their professional association."

— **Alan Sauer**, CAE, IOM, Fellow, American Society of Association Executives, and former Chair of the Board of Trustees, U.S. Chamber of Commerce Institute for Organization Management

"This book happens to hit on one of my hot buttons. I have made numerous speeches on communication, which I consider the common denominator of success or failure. Invariably, people do not reflect on body language as a means of communication until you bring it to their attention. *The Nonverbal Advantage* should be a great success!"

— **Charles A. Lynch**, Chair, Market Value Partners Company

"Face-to-face communication takes on a new meaning in this much-needed and detailed treatise on nonverbal communication. Understanding how humans give silent clues—with eyes, hands, posture, and even feet—helps us become better speakers and better listeners.

— **Wilma Mathews**, ABC, IABC Fellow, Faculty Associate, Walter Cronkite School of Journalism and Mass Communication, and Communication Consultant

"Carol Kinsey Goman shows you how to use body language skills to build stronger professional relationships. *The Nonverbal Advantage* is a must-read for anyone wanting to move ahead and stand out from the crowd."

— **Robert L. Dilenschneider**, Founder and Principal, The Dilenschneider Group, and author of *Power and Influence: The Rules Have Changed*

"In my global business dealings, I've seen negotiations fall apart when people gave the wrong signals and didn't respect cultural differences. *The Nonverbal Advantage* should be required reading for anyone in sales or negotiations—especially if they work internationally."

> — **Kimberly Benson**, Vice President, Cange International, Inc.

"In a brave new world brimming with discovery and invention, we must remember to update our existing human-insights skill set. Now is the time to renew your toolbox by including knowledge of the nonverbal cues that will take center stage in business and in life. Carol Kinsey Goman's book is a timely read indeed."

> — **Watts Wacker**, futurist and coauthor of *What's Your Story? Storytelling to Move Markets, Audiences, People, and Brands*

"*The Nonverbal Advantage* is a fresh look at employee communication management and the more subtle, but nevertheless important, cues of body language. Goman's analysis of interpersonal communication techniques, signals, and behaviors suggests that nonverbal signals are more important in understanding human behavior than words alone— the nonverbal 'channels' seem to be more powerful than what people say. She is pointing the way for managers at all levels."

> — **Deborah Radman**, APR, Fellow PRSA,
> Senior Vice President/Director, CKPR

"In the second half of my thirty-three-year career in law enforcement, my interview ability and success took a definite upswing after taking training that addressed not only verbal deception but also nonverbal behavior. Carol's book takes many of the things I learned about body language and puts them in a form that any manager or business professional can use."

> — **Robert Baker**, retired San Diego County District Attorney
> Investigator and San Diego County Sheriff Detective

*The Nonverbal
Advantage*

The Nonverbal Advantage

Secrets and Science of Body Language at Work

Carol Kinsey Goman

BK

Berrett–Koehler Publishers, Inc.
San Francisco
a BK Business book

Berrett-Koehler Publishers, Inc.
235 Montgomery Street, Suite 650, San Francisco, CA 94104-2916
Tel: (415) 288-0260   Fax: (415) 362-2512   www.bkconnection.com

Ordering Information

Quantity sales. Special discounts are available on quantity purchases by corporations, associations, and others. For details, contact the "Special Sales Department" at the Berrett-Koehler address above.

Individual sales. Berrett-Koehler publications are available through most bookstores. They can also be ordered directly from Berrett-Koehler:
Tel: (800) 929-2929; Fax: (802) 864-7626; www.bkconnection.com.

Orders for college textbook/course adoption use. Please contact Berrett-Koehler:
Tel: (800) 929-2929; Fax: (802) 864-7626.

Orders by U.S. trade bookstores and wholesalers. Please contact Ingram Publisher Services, Tel: (800) 509-4887; Fax: (800) 838-1149; E-mail: customer.service@ingrampublisherservices.com; or visit www.ingrampublisher services.com/Ordering for details about electronic ordering.

Berrett-Koehler and the BK logo are registered trademarks of Berrett-Koehler Publishers, Inc.

Printed in the United States of America

Berrett-Koehler books are printed on long-lasting acid-free paper. When it is available, we choose paper that has been manufactured by environmentally responsible processes. These may include using trees grown in sustainable forests, incorporating recycled paper, minimizing chlorine in bleaching, or recycling the energy produced at the paper mill.

Library of Congress Cataloging-in-Publication Data

Goman, Carol Kinsey.
    The nonverbal advantage : secrets and science of body language at work / Carol Kinsey Goman.
        p. cm.
    Includes index.
    ISBN 978-1-57675-492-4 (pbk. : alk. paper)
    1. Body language. 2. Nonverbal communication in the workplace. I. Title.

BF637.N66G66 2008
650.1'3—dc22
2007052581

13 12 11 10 09 08   10 9 8 7 6 5 4 3 2 1

Interior design and composition by Gary Palmatier, Ideas to Images.
Elizabeth von Radics, copyeditor; Mike Mollett, proofreader; Medea Minnich, indexer.

Dedication

To Skip because I love him,
to Joyce because she's always in my corner,
and to Toni because she's my best friend and favorite sister

Contents

The most important thing in communication is hearing what isn't said.
—Peter F. Drucker

Introduction

Hᴀᴠᴇ ʏᴏᴜ ᴇᴠᴇʀ ᴡᴏɴᴅᴇʀᴇᴅ...

What kind of impression am I making?

Should I believe what my boss told me?

Am I dealing with a potential buyer, or am I just wasting my time?

Did my whole team understand what I said?

What did the customer mean by that?

How do I know if he really supports my idea?

Is the audience angry, frustrated, interested, or bored?

The answers to such questions are right before your eyes. That's because people in professional settings are constantly telling each other exactly what they think and feel—and it often has nothing to do with the words they speak. Your boss may say that you'll be considered for a promotion, but if she's leaning back with crossed arms and a forced smile, she's sending the opposite message. The customer may say he's not interested in buying that new car, but if he keeps glancing at the contract on the table, he's telling you that he *is* interested.

The silent signals of nonverbal communication tend to reveal underlying motives and emotions—fear, honesty, joy, indecision, frustration—and much more. The tiniest gestures, like the way your co-workers stand or enter a room, often speak volumes about their confidence, self-worth, and credibility. And the way *you* sit, stand, or look at others reveals more about your true intent than you may realize.

Body Language Expertise

I've been an expert at using body language from the day I was born. You may be surprised to learn that you have been, too. As infants we displayed a variety of facial expressions to signal our moods and needs, pointed at objects of interest, and bonded with our mothers through the power of eye contact. As children we assimilated those gestures and expressions that were appropriate in our families and in our cultures. Then, as we grew older, we learned to refine (and disguise) signals that were too obvious or unwelcome.

We did most of this unconsciously.

It wasn't until I was in a master's program in college, preparing to be a therapist, that I became aware of the nonverbal signals that I'd been sending and receiving all my life. Training in Neuro-Linguistic Programming and Ericksonian approaches to hypnosis and psychotherapy taught me how to observe people's eye movements, facial expressions, and body postures to discover their inner motivation and resistance. When I began consulting to business organizations and speaking to national and then international audiences, I paid more attention to my own body language so that the gestures, postures, and expressions I used would accurately reflect the message I wanted to get across. I use these same insights and techniques with the executives and managers I now coach.

As I began doing research for this book, I learned of the most recent advances in the field. Scientists from evolutionary psychology, neurobiology, medicine, sociology, criminology, anthropology, and communication studies have all brought their methods and concepts to the field of nonverbal communication. The result is a deeper understanding of *how* and *why* body language is so powerful.

Body Language in the Workplace

A thorough understanding of the role that body language plays in our day-to-day business activities is vital. And yet I see it time and again: executives, managers, and salespeople who aren't reading the clear signals of others or who don't have a clue how their own nonverbal communication is sabotaging their efforts. At a time when it is widely recognized that professional success is achieved with or through other people, the power of, and the need for, good interpersonal skills couldn't be greater. My goal with this book is to help you optimize the power of nonverbal communication in your professional life.

"I take time to lick the customer's face; I wag my tail when they talk; I jump up and down when they walk through the door. That's what sets me apart from all the other salespeople!"

On the other hand, those who have mastered these skills—not only to accurately decode the silent signals of others but also to use body language that is aligned with the attitudes they want to project—gain a competitive advantage in business. And that applies to whatever business they are in!

If you are among America's 2.3 million executives, 4.3 million salespeople, 6.8 million waiters, 735,000 lawyers, 567,000 doctors, 212,000 coaches, 842,000 police officers, 3.8 million teachers, 1 million security guards—or everyone else who deals with the public, makes presentations, or negotiates with or manages people—your professional success is tightly linked to your use and knowledge of body language.

The following are just a few examples of that link in action.

Leadership The effectiveness of command-and-control management tactics declined dramatically with the end of the Industrial Age. Today's leaders, whether chief executives or first-line supervisors, must lead through influence rather than rely on the control (or the illusion of control) that a management position implies.

Influence relies on two things:

- the ability to really understand the employee's perspective, which in turn means listening to what's being said *and* knowing how to read the messages that are being delivered nonverbally; and

- the ability to communicate congruently, to align the spoken word with body language that supports, instead of sabotages, an intended message.

Education When it comes to motivating students to complete their work, nonverbal behavior is a prime factor in teacher effectiveness. Research studies with fifth-grade, high school, and college students found that learners at all levels reacted more favorably to teachers who used nonverbal *immediacy cues:* eye contact, affirmative head nodding, leaning forward, and smiling. Increasing immediacy behaviors dramatically improves students' motivation, how much they like a class, and their willingness to follow the teacher's or professor's recommendation.

Sales The moment salespeople meet prospective customers, the customers are being judged by how they look and what they do. The process takes about seven seconds, but the impression lasts. Making or breaking a sale often depends on the nonverbal signals that are exchanged during this initial contact. Attire, body positions, expressions, facial movements, and eye contact are all factors to be understood and managed by the successful salesperson.

Negotiation Masterful negotiation results from being able to correctly read between the lines of what people are saying. One of the most powerful ways to do this is to acquire an understanding of body language. Effective negotiators recognize when they need to slow down or speed up the negotiation process. They know how to relieve anxiety and calm difficult situations. Rather than relying solely on verbal cues, however, the primary way they gauge what is happening is by watching for nonverbal behavior that signals someone's unconscious, and therefore unmonitored, motivation.

Healthcare The relationship between physicians' nonverbal communication skills and their patients' satisfaction with medical care is substantial. Although the physicians' nonverbal communication skills won't affect patients' ratings of the technical quality of care, doctors who are more sensitive to nonverbal cues and who express what the Medical College of Virginia calls "clinical empathy" create higher overall patient satisfaction—and are sued less often!

Law enforcement   When interrogating suspects, instead of just listening for inconsistencies in what is said, trained police officers look for minute physical reactions on the faces of people being questioned, such as fleeting smiles that may indicate when a suspect believes he has fooled a questioner.

Customer service   It has long been believed that a positive attitude among employees is key to the effective delivery of customer service. Research shows that an employee's ability to detect nonverbal cues is just as important. An employee who is adept at reading body language is better equipped to identify what customers are truly thinking or feeling.

Virtually Yours

If a business leader is going to talk about new initiatives, strategic opportunities, or organizational transformations—or if he or she has to deliver bad news—my advice is to do so face to face. Likewise, if a team (even one that is geographically dispersed) is about to embark on a collaboration, I would advise beginning that process with an in-person meeting that allows team members to get to know one another.

In face-to-face interactions, our brains process a continuous cascade of nonverbal cues that we use as the basis for building trust and professional intimacy—both of which are critical to high-level collaboration. No such subliminal interpretation takes place with e-mail or other electronic discussion forums.

Until recently, that lack of subliminal interpretation in communication technology included videoconferences, but now Cisco Systems is one of several companies (Hewlett-Packard and Apple are two others) working on products that make the virtual experience almost the same as a face-to-face

***Cisco's TelePresence Meeting is the next
best thing to being there.***

interaction. I saw an amazing demonstration of Cisco's Tele-Presence Meeting. Using life-size high-definition video and directional sound technology, this new generation of video-conferencing makes participants like they are actually sitting in the same room with people who are on the other side of the world (or, in my case, across the Cisco campus in San Jose, California). Best of all, I was able to make eye contact with my virtual partners, and we could respond to each other's expressions and gestures.

Videoconferencing is just one aspect of a larger visual technology revolution that includes *vlogs* (video blogs—the frequent publishing of videos on the Web, featuring stream-of-consciousness content) and video-sharing Web sites such as YouTube. What this means for business professionals who used to hide behind their computer monitors is that they will soon be *viewed* instead of *read*. And they will need to sharpen their nonverbal communication skills.

Chapters Outline

This book presents a subject that I have found to be fascinating and valuable throughout my professional life. You'll find photographs, cartoons, "Try This" suggestions, and real-life workplace examples. And, of course, in every chapter you'll discover the secrets of effective body language with the science that backs them up.

Chapter 1: The Five *C*'s of Body Language lays a framework for the book by giving an overview of factors—context, clusters, congruence, consistency, and culture—that need to be considered when decoding the messages in someone's body language.

The next five chapters take you through the body from head to toe. **Chapter 2: Reading the Whole Body** looks at emotional body language, physical postures, posing, and leanings to show how the entire body communicates. **Chapter 3: The Eyes Have It** explains the power of eye contact, gives general definitions for a variety of eye movements, and shows how to tell the difference between a business gaze and a social gaze. **Chapter 4: Face to Face** covers facial expressions and the emotions behind them. Included are the six expressions that are universally recognized and understood (joy, sadness, surprise, fear, disgust/contempt, and anger), how to tell a real smile from a fake one, and the meaning behind head positions. **Chapter 5: Talking with Your Hands** looks at hand and arm gestures and shows how they play a part in displaying confidence, openness, resistance, and anxiety. **Chapter 6: Feet First** explores the fascinating body language of the feet and the legs—parts of the body where gestures often go unnoticed.

Chapter 7: You're in My Space looks at spatial zones—those distances between people that are most appropriate for intimate, personal, social, and public interactions. In this chapter you'll learn why seating arrangements are so important in business meetings and what someone's office can tell you about the person.

Chapter 8: The Power of Touch examines touch cues, with special emphasis on the elements of an effective business handshake. It also looks at "touching etiquette" in the workplace and why even a momentary touch can create a human bond.

Chapter 9: Translating Body Language across Cultures looks at some of the cultural differences in nonverbal communication. From greeting behaviors to hand gestures to the use of personal space to body postures and touch, what feels right in one culture may be ineffective or even offensive in another.

Chapter 10: Selling Your Message without Saying a Word lets you see how others are interpreting your body language signals. You'll learn how to make a positive impression in that crucial first seven seconds of meeting someone, how to project your natural charisma, and how to be more confident leading team meetings or giving business presentations.

One note: If you think that body language skills are a way to fool or manipulate people, you may be surprised to learn that it's just the opposite. The nonverbal advantage lies in learning how to use body language to enhance sincere messages of candor, caring, and rapport. You can't fake sincerity—at least not for very long. But then, neither can anyone else.

Skill Building

Using nonverbal communication as a business tool means becoming conscious of what was previously a mostly unconscious process. Instead of just having a feeling about someone, you can learn which body signals led you to that insight—and then decide whether your conclusion was valid. Instead of just hoping you are making a good impression, you can learn the nonverbal signals of confidence and credibility.

Mastering this essential set of professional skills is not a matter of learning something new; rather it's becoming aware of how powerful nonverbal communication is and honing your innate instincts and talents to better harness that power. This means you can become more proficient at understanding and projecting body language in a single reading of this book. And with practice you will be able to improve the reliability of your first impressions; decode eye, facial, and body gestures with conviction; quickly build rapport with clients and team members; understand what people are reading in your body language; and take control of the nonverbal messages you are sending.

Best of all—it's fun! You can sharpen your skills while waiting at the airport, during a business meeting or family dinner, or at a party with your friends. You'll be amazed at the insights you'll gain into what the body language of others is saying to you—and how much you'll learn about your own nonverbal signals. And when you apply these new insights to your professional relationships, you'll find that the nonverbal advantage becomes a key to business success.

CHAPTER 1

The Five C's of Body Language

BODY LANGUAGE IS LIKE A COMPUTER. We all know what it is, but most of us are never exactly sure how it works. That's because the process of receiving and decoding non-verbal communication is often done without our conscious awareness. It simply happens. Human beings are genetically programmed to look for facial and behavioral cues and to quickly understand their meaning. We see someone gesture and automatically make a judgment about the intention of that gesture.

And we've been doing this for a long, long time. As a species we knew how to win friends and influence people—or avoid/placate/confront those we couldn't befriend—long before we knew how to use words. Our ancestors made survival decisions based solely on intricate bits of visual information they were picking up from others. And they did so quickly. In our prehistory, rapidly deciding if a situation or person was dangerous was often a matter of life or death.

There is a world of information you can learn about people simply by observing how they use their bodies to send nonverbal cues. But to accurately decode those signals, you need to interrupt your automatic judgment system and analyze your impressions. To uncover its true meaning, body language needs to be understood in context, viewed in clusters, evaluated for congruence with what is being said, assessed for consistency, and filtered for cultural influences. This chapter shows you how to do that.

Filtering Your First Impressions: The Five C's

Nonverbal signals play a key role in helping us form quick impressions. Our ability to do so is one of our basic survival instincts. But, as innate as this ability may be, not all our first impressions are accurate. Although our brains are hardwired to respond instantly to certain nonverbal cues, that circuitry was put in place a long time ago—when our ancient ancestors faced threats and challenges that were very different from those we face in today's modern society. Life is more complex today, with layers of social restrictions and nuanced meanings adding to the intricacies of our interpersonal dealings. This is especially true in workplace settings, where corporate culture adds its own complexities—a unique set of restrictions and guidelines for behavior.

Although first impressions may not always be accurate, you can improve your ability to read someone's body language by filtering your impressions through the five C's: context, clusters, congruence, consistency, and culture.

Context

Imagine this scene: It's a freezing-cold winter evening with a light snow falling and a north wind blowing. You see a woman—you realize it's a co-worker—sitting on a bench at a bus stop. Her head is down, her eyes are tightly closed, and she's hunched over, shivering slightly and hugging herself.

Now the scene changes: It's the same woman in the same physical position. But instead of sitting outdoors on a bench, she's seated behind her desk in the office next to yours. Her body language is identical: head down, eyes closed, hunched over, shivering, and hugging herself. The nonverbal signals are the same, but the new setting has altered your perception of those signals. In a flash she's gone from telling you, "I'm really cold!" to saying, "I'm in distress."

The meaning of nonverbal communication changes as the context changes. Just like in real estate, location matters. We can't begin to understand someone's behavior without considering the circumstances under which the behavior occurred. As illustrated by our example, the message sent by that woman's body language changed dramatically depending on whether she was sitting outside in the cold or alone in her office. And some situations require more-formal behaviors that might be interpreted very differently in any other setting.

When people are interacting, their relationship determines much of the context. The same man talking with a client, his boss, or a subordinate may display very different body language with each. Time of day, expectations based on past encounters, and whether the interaction is taking place in a private or public setting—all these variables form the context in which body language occurs, and they need to be taken into consideration when you evaluate meaning. The key is to judge if the nonverbal behaviors are appropriate to the context in which they occur.

For example, Dave and Diane had been friends and colleagues for years. As such they stood close to each other, maintained strong eye contact, touched one another on the arm, and smiled often during their workplace conversations. No one thought to comment on this until Diane announced her engagement to another employee in the same company. Armed with that information, the next time a co-worker saw Dave and Diane smiling and enjoying each other's company, he said, "Careful now, she's engaged!"

The relationship context had suddenly changed. Apparently, nonverbal behavior that was deemed appropriate for Dave when Diane was "single," was now viewed as a potential problem.

TRY THIS

Choose one nonverbal behavior (say, touching a colleague on the arm) and list all the conditions under which the behavior would be acceptable in your company or organization. Now list all the contextual changes that might make this gesture inappropriate. Ask yourself how changing the physical location (in a private office, in a meeting room with several colleagues, on-stage when being presented an award, or in the hallway when involved in casual conversation) could alter the meaning of the gesture. How could the status of the individuals involved or the quality of their relationship change the nonverbal message being sent?

Clusters

Nonverbal cues occur in a *gesture cluster*—a group of movements, postures, and actions that reinforce a common point. A single gesture can have several meanings or mean nothing at all (sometimes a cigar *is* just a cigar), but when you couple that single gesture with other nonverbal signals, the meaning becomes clearer. A person may cross her arms for any number of reasons, but when the gesture is coupled with a scowl, a headshake, and legs turned away from you, you have a composite picture and reinforcement to conclude that she is resistant to whatever you just proposed.

Always remember to look for clusters of behaviors. A person's overall demeanor is far more telling than a single gesture viewed independently.

A savvy manager I know begins every staff meeting by taking off his jacket, and he chooses a chair at the center of the conference table (not at the head). Those behaviors alone would send a message of informality, but it's the rest of his gestures that drive the point home. Whenever anyone in the meeting speaks, the manager leans forward with an expression of interest on his face, nods approvingly, and gives the speaker full eye contact. This cluster of gestures symbolically sets the stage for exactly what he wants the meeting to be—a rank-free exchange of ideas and questions.

TRY THIS

Count to three. That is, refrain from assuming that any single gesture has a particular meaning until you see two corroborating gestures that reinforce that same meaning.

Congruence

A classic study by Dr. Albert Mehrabian at the University of California at Los Angeles found that the *total impact* of a message is based on 7 percent words used, 38 percent tone of voice, and 55 percent facial expressions, hand gestures, body position, and other forms of nonverbal communication.

Obviously, you can't watch a person speaking in a foreign language and understand 93 percent of what is being communicated. (Mehrabian was studying only the communication of *feelings*—particularly the feelings of like and dislike.) Still, you can bet that when the verbal and nonverbal channels of communication are out of sync, people—especially women—tend to rely on the nonverbal message and disregard the verbal content.

When thoughts and words are in tune (that is, when people believe what they are saying), you see it corroborated in their body language. Their gestures and expressions are in alignment with what is being said.

You also see *incongruence,* where gestures contradict words: a side-to-side headshake while saying yes or someone frowning and staring at the ground while telling you she is happy. Incongruence is a sign not so much of intentional deceit but of inner conflict between what someone is thinking and what he or she is saying.

I noticed this conflict in Sheila, a manager I was coaching. Sheila appeared calm and reasonable as she listed the reasons why she should delegate more responsibility to her staff. But every time she expressed these opinions, she also (almost imperceptibly) shuddered. While Sheila's words declared her intention of empowering her employees, the quick, involuntary shudder was saying loud and clear, "I don't want to do this!"

TRY THIS

Here's an exercise that I suggest practicing *outside* of your workplace: Whenever someone asks you a question that can be answered with a simple yes or no (for example, "Would you like fries with that?"), answer in the affirmative while subtly shaking your head from side to side. Then watch how others react to the incongruence in your response.

Consistency

You need to know a person's *baseline* behavior under relaxed or generally stress-free conditions so that you can compare it with the expressions and the gestures that appear when that person is under stress. What is his normal way of looking around, of sitting, of standing when relaxed? How does he respond when discussing some nonthreatening topic? Knowing someone's behavioral baseline enhances your ability to spot meaningful deviations.

One of the strategies that experienced police interrogators use for spotting dishonesty is to ask a series of nonthreatening questions while observing how the subject behaves when there is no reason to lie. Then, when the more difficult issues get addressed, the officers watch for changes in nonverbal behavior that indicate deception around key points.

TRY THIS

The best way to understand someone's baseline behavior is to observe him over an extended period of time. So, when you interact with your business colleagues, begin to notice—*really* notice—how they look when they are relaxed and comfortable. How much eye contact do they make? What kind of gestures do they use? What body postures do they assume?

Then, once you know what is normal for your co-workers, you will be able to quickly and accurately detect even minor shifts when their body language behavior is out of character.

We all run into problems trying to evaluate the consistency of someone we've just met. The following is an example of something that happened to me a few years ago.

I was giving a presentation to the chief executive officer (CEO) of a financial services company, outlining a speech I was scheduled to deliver to his leadership team the next day. And it wasn't going well. Our meeting lasted almost an hour, and through that entire time the CEO sat at the conference table with his arms tightly crossed. He didn't once smile or nod in encouragement. When I finished, he said, "Thank you" (without making eye contact) and left the room.

As I'm a body language *expert,* I was sure that his nonverbal communication was telling me that my speaking engagement would be canceled. But when I walked to the elevator, the CEO's assistant came up to me to tell me how impressed her boss had been with my presentation. I was shocked and asked how he would have reacted had he *not* liked it. "Oh," said the assistant, her smile acknowledging that she had previously seen that reaction as well. "He would have gotten up in the middle of your presentation and walked out!"

The only nonverbal signals that I had received from that CEO were ones I judged to be negative. What I didn't realize was that, for this individual, that was normal behavior.

Culture

All nonverbal communication is influenced by our cultural heritage, which is discussed at length in chapter 9. For now it's important to understand that when reading body language you should consider the amount of stress the person is under. That's because the higher the emotional level, the more likely it is that culture-specific gestures will show up.

In addition, body language is affected by the many subcultures of which we're a part. Take posture, for example. Ballet dancers are trained to hold their bodies chest-forward, so you'll often see them standing like this with their heels together and toes pointed out (a modified first position). Many office workers are round-shouldered with a slight slump in the chest from hours spent hunched over their keyboards. Military personnel often carry a shoulders-back, spine-straight stance long after their tour of duty has concluded.

People from different regions of the same country may also use their bodies very differently. Take, for example, the fast-paced stride of a typical New Yorker and contrast it with the more leisurely gait of someone from the South. Or think of the potential body language differences between a prototypically reserved and formal New Englander and his more casual California counterpart.

The more you know about a person's background, hobbies, and interests, the more you can understand why certain gestures or postures are part of her unique repertoire—and why deviation from these patterns is significant. Sometimes people shift postures as they shift subjects. In my therapy practice, I would often see patients assume one posture when talking about their mother and a completely different posture when discussing their father.

TRY THIS

Choose one business colleague and make a list of everything you know about her background, including her ethnic heritage, where she was born and raised, her hobbies, her family, and the sports or physical activities she enjoys. Once you have a full list, start observing your co-worker to see if you can spot the nonverbal cues that are a result of some part of her background.

Keep in mind the five C's—context, clusters, congruence, consistency, and culture—as you go through the rest of this book. There is no doubt that people use nonverbal communication to reveal their state of mind. But reading body language isn't just about learning nonverbal signals; it is also about understanding how to get to the real meaning behind those signals.

CHAPTER 2

Reading the Whole Body

KINESICS **IS THE TERM** that refers to body movements and the meanings they communicate. By paying careful attention to a variety of body movements—such as posture, leanings, and breathing patterns—and noticing when someone makes a sudden transition from one position to another, you can get a good idea of the other person's shifting mood and attitude. In this chapter you'll see how body movements send their unique messages. You'll also learn why *mirroring*—a communication technique of mimicking another person's posture and gestures—is a powerful way to build rapport.

Emotional Body Language

In the past, scientists thought that human emotions were mainly read and transferred through facial expressions. New research from the field of cognitive and affective neuroscience suggests that whole-body signals can be just as significant in emotional communication and decision-making. This connection is especially powerful when it involves fear. A person's expression may convey to you that there's a threat, but it gives you no information about how to react to the threat. (Should you fight, flee, or freeze?) Emotional body language shows what other people are *doing* in response to the fear.

The findings also suggest that the immediate response to other people's fear may be more automatic than previously thought. The results may help explain how fear spreads—as the immediate, but unconscious, response to others' fear.

Is your organization going through a major change—downsizing, reorganization, or acquisition? If so, you have been exposed to (and have reacted to) other employees' fear. And your emotional reaction may have led to decisions and actions that you later justified by rational thinking. The more you become aware of this powerful, instantaneous link, the more you gain insight into your own behavior and that of your co-workers.

We're Wired to Connect

Nonverbal communication has been the subject of extensive research over the past several years, yet some of the most interesting findings come when least expected. One such finding came from a laboratory in Italy, where scientists were studying the brain cells of macaque monkeys.

Researchers had confirmed that when a monkey performs a single highly specific hand action, neurons in the motor cortex are very active. For example, every time a monkey reached for a peanut, certain cells on either side of its brain "fired," creating a buzzing sound that was detectable by highly sophisticated monitoring equipment.

One day a monkey wired up for such an experiment happened to see a human grab a peanut. Much to the researchers' surprise, the same neurons fired in the same way. In terms of motor cell activity, the monkey's brain *could not tell the difference between actually doing something and seeing it done.* Because the cells reflected the actions that the monkey observed in others, the neuroscientists named them "mirror neurons."

Later experiments confirmed the existence of mirror neurons in humans. This system of neurons allows the brain to perform its highest tasks, including learning and imitating. But the research revealed another surprise. For human beings, in addition to mirroring actions, the cells reflected sensations and feelings.

Ever wonder why when someone near you yawns you also yawn? Or why you cringe when you see another person getting a vaccination? Turns out it's your mirror neurons at work. The moment you see an emotion expressed on someone's face—or read it in her gestures or posture—you unconsciously place yourself in the other person's "mental shoes" and begin to sense that same emotion within yourself. For this reason mirror neurons are sometimes referred to as Dalai Lama neurons because they provide a biological basis for compassion.

Matters of the Heart

One way that people show their emotions is by shifts in the chest. Some of these movements are subtle; others are more obvious, but, large or small, they are always revealing. The heart, brain, and nervous system are so closely interlocked that you can often tell whether someone is happy or depressed by simply observing how he holds his chest. A promotion may have a person walking around with his chest "puffed out with pride"; an acute disappointment may result in rounded shoulders and a concave chest—the look of someone "kicked in the stomach." It's also been noted that when men are comfortable with their surroundings, they unbutton their jackets (an unconscious gesture that removes a barrier to showing their hearts?).

The metaphors we use to describe emotional experiences connected with the heart are, in fact, perhaps most revealing of all. "Her heart sank." "He was heartsick about it." These aren't just descriptive phrases; they are based on physiological fact. (The National Institute for Mental Health posits a direct link between depression and heart problems.)

On the positive side, we use phrases like "His heart was in his throat" to describe the heart-pumping combination of adrenaline and endorphins that flood us in moments of elation as the sympathetic nervous system gets charged and ready for action. When people are excited and happy, they fill up with those good feelings. Look for a sudden upper-body shift—usually upward and forward—and a big inhalation.

A display of very good feelings

The Breath of Life

When you inhale, you are literally feeding yourself. The human organism can go weeks without food and days without water yet only a few minutes without air. You knew that, of course. But did you know that *how* you breathe reveals a lot about your emotional state?

For example: Holding one's breath is a primitive instinct— a self-protection mechanism (part of the "freeze" component in the fight, flight, or freeze response) when hiding from a predator. Today, even though predators are more symbolic, any anxiety can cause a person to hold his breath or to breathe in small, shallow breaths. (On polygraph exams, people who are going to lie tend to stop breathing, and it shows up on the machine.)

Shallow breathing is also a strong signal of low confidence. If a speaker is taking shallow breaths while trying to give a pep talk, regardless of how well spoken she is, listeners find it difficult to believe anything she says. And one person's shallow-breathing pattern can affect other people's emotional states as well. The natural tendency of people to mirror and adopt the rhythms of those around them extends to breathing rates. Without any of the parties being aware of how it happened, a shallow breather can make an entire room feel anxious.

TRY THIS

When you're talking with your co-workers, watch their breathing patterns. Pay attention to how deeply or shallowly people breathe and notice how you respond to the different breathing patterns. If you're in a group, notice how a deep inhalation often signals that a person is about to speak, and the entire group will unconsciously pick up the signal and turn toward that person.

Body Postures: Closed and Open

I recently addressed a group of managers from a major international firm about the importance of interpersonal business skills. All the managers actively participated in the session, asking questions and volunteering answers. All, that is, except one woman who sat for the entire session with her shoulders rounded, head tilted forward, and body twisted slightly toward the exit. At the end of the program, she said, "I'm not really a 'people person.' I'm just not comfortable with this touchy-feely stuff." But of course I already knew that. And so did everyone else in the room. The woman's body language had been shouting out her discomfort all morning.

In *closed* body postures, arms are folded, legs are crossed, and the entire body is usually turned away. Lower status is often shown by bowing the head (a subservient gesture) and holding the body to make it appear smaller (and less of a threat) than it actually is. Rounding the upper body and hiding the hands are closed signs that also represent feelings of vulnerability. Remember, of course, that there are no absolutes associated with any of these conclusions. A man who hides his hands, for example, may also mean that he is just embarrassed about the appearance of his fingernails.

In *open* and receptive body postures, legs are uncrossed and arms are open with palms exposed. If the arms are relaxed at the sides of the body, this is also generally a sign of openness, accessibility, and an overall willingness to interact.

More predictably than their male counterparts, women—when sitting—adopt an open-arm posture in the presence of someone they

She's open to you and your ideas.

like, and they tend to fold their arms across their chest when they feel indifferent to or dislike the other person.

Two things I know for sure about open and closed postures:

- Individuals with open body positions are perceived more positively than those with closed body positions.

- Individuals with open body positions are more persuasive than those with closed body positions.

TRY THIS

Compare the body language of your co-workers. Watch the people who are the most convincing and successful. I bet you'll find that they typically use open body positions when interacting with colleagues and presenting their ideas.

Body posture may also show someone's status in a group. I've seen meetings where all subordinates slumped, while the leader assumed a more erect posture that indicated his dominance. (I've also watched two executives of similar heights meeting for the first time and saw both men straighten their postures and stretch their bodies to emphasize their respective heights.) These positions were taken without any of the participants' being aware of their postures. But sometimes awareness *does* play a role. People of equal status tend to mirror one another, but people of high status may deliberately adopt a different posture to show that they are not just one of the gang.

A posture that Charles, Prince of Wales, often assumes—head held high, chin out, and one palm holding the other hand behind his back—is a high-confidence pose. The person assuming this posture exposes the entire front of his or her body—as an unconscious act of fearlessness or superiority.

Leanings

Positive attitudes toward others tend to be accompanied by leaning forward—especially when sitting down.

When two people like each other, you'll see them both lean in. In groups, outsiders typically stand with their weight on one foot, while those who are really "in" lean forward a little and tip their heads forward. Research shows that individuals who lean forward tend to increase the verbal output of the person with whom they're speaking.

An agent with the federal Bureau of Alcohol, Tobacco, and Firearms admitted to using this strategy when questioning a suspect. "When it looks as if the suspect is going to confess," he told me, "I lean toward him. I might even touch his arm. This creates an intimacy that allows for the suspect to confess in a whisper instead of a 'room voice.' It also allows me to speak in a lower, more compassionate tone of voice."

Leaning in to connect

TRY THIS

If you use leaning as a business technique, be aware that leaning toward a person in the early stages of a conversation will generally be perceived as encroaching on his territory. Early leans can make people uncomfortable and *decrease* their perception of you as likable. So wait until you've developed a level of rapport and interpersonal comfort, *then* make your move.

Leaning backward usually signals feelings of dislike or negativity. It's a hardwired response from the limbic brain; we subconsciously try to distance ourselves from anyone or anything that is unpleasant, disagreeable, or dangerous. In a seated conversation, leaning backward can also communicate dominance.

Leaning away to distance himself

When viewed as part of a cluster, different combinations of body tilts and open or closed postures can signal these generalized meanings:

- Leaning back with a closed body posture can show disinterest or disagreement.

- Leaning back with an open body posture can indicate contemplation.

- Leaning forward with a closed body posture can signal hostility.

- Leaning forward with an open body posture can show interest or agreement.

- Leaning sideways (and slightly back) with asymmetrical arm and leg positions and loosely held hands can be a sign of relaxation and ease. I've also noticed that people tend to engage in more sideways leans when interacting with lower-status individuals than with higher-status individuals.

TRY THIS

With everyone you encounter, visualize them as a traffic signal. If the person is displaying open postures and gestures, think of this as a green light to proceed with your interaction. If the person's body sends signals of disbelief or defensiveness (yellow light), you'll know to slow down and advance with caution. Defiant closed positions accompanied by facial scowls are the equivalent of a red stoplight—and your cue to back off or try an entirely new approach.

When He Has All the Answers

Someone feeling confident or superior will often sit, leaning back with his hands behind his head and his fingers interlocked (this is a mostly masculine gesture).

Because it can be irritating to deal with someone with this "I have all the answers" posture, there are a couple of ways to counteract it. You can mirror the gesture, which will show agreement ("We think alike") and hopefully put the person at ease. Or, if the person using the hands-behind-the-head gesture is trying to intimidate you, your matching posture will be seen as a nonverbal challenge to his know-it-all attitude. You can also encourage him to change position by handing him something so that he has to move his hands from behind his head and lean forward to accept the item.

Confidence or superiority

Bodies under Stress

Fundamentally, there are two kinds of nonverbal signals that people send: one that shows someone is comfortable and another that indicates some level of anxiety or stress. Except for the rare sociopath, deception is generally accompanied by stress, which is often manifested in closed and defensive postures such as crossing one's arms, with palms hidden, and leaning away from a questioner.

Nervousness or excitement, positive or negative, is often displayed as excessive movement. When people are very agitated, they can't seem to stay in one position. Their hands may tremble, they may perspire excessively (especially on the upper lip), or, when standing, they may rock from one leg to another. For many the ultimate stereotype of this behavior is the worried baseball manager pacing back and forth in the dugout. For others it is the poker player who leaks nonverbal "tells" about the hand he was dealt.

Rufus had mastered the poker face.
The poker tail, on the other hand...

Hands on Hips

The little girl in the grocery store was having none of it. Her mother's promise of "pizza as soon as we finish shopping" was failing to make an impression. The girl wanted pizza and she wanted it *now*! There she stood, feet firmly planted shoulder-width apart and hands balled in tight little fists on her hips.

You've seen this gesture too. Often. Whether in a stubborn toddler or a defiant adult, hands on hips is one of the most common gestures people use to communicate an aggressive, superconfident, or independent attitude.

The stance of defiance

Remember that, like every other gesture, it is important to look for clusters and to consider the circumstances in which the gesture takes place—its context. Hands on hips and a tapping foot from a man waiting for his co-worker to finish a report may be more a sign of frustration with the delay than of real anger. But if you also notice that the man's jacket is open (a fearless pose that exposes the front of his body), his hands are on his hips, and he is squared off in front of his co-worker with an angry facial expression, you would be justified in concluding that the situation has escalated beyond mere irritation.

Seated Readiness

People often signal that they are ready to end a conversation by assuming the position of someone ready to rise. They may move to the edge of the chair, or they may lean forward with their hands on the arms of the chair or on their knees. If you are aware of someone assuming these postures while you are speaking, you should read that signal and quickly finish what you are saying.

TRY THIS

If you're in sales, this tip is for you. A research team videotaped insurance salespeople interviewing potential buyers and found this fascinating correlation: If the customer displayed a chin-stroking gesture (the decision-making signal) and followed it by a crossed-arms position, the sale was off. But if chin stroking was followed by this seated readiness position, the client almost always bought the policy.

So be on the lookout for the chin stroke and seated-readiness cluster of gestures. When you spot it, go for the close!

Body Orientation

The degree to which someone's legs and shoulders face the direction of someone else indicates the level of liking or the status of that person. The more someone's body orientation is toward you, the better your chances that the other person has a positive attitude about you. When you see people turn their bodies away from you, you've probably lost their interest. In fact, orienting away from someone almost always conveys detachment or boredom regardless of the words spoken.

But orienting your body directly toward another person can also be off-putting. Standing in a squared-off position—"toe to toe"—may be equated with confrontation. Imagine the body positions of two men just before they fight. Or picture the baseball manager who was pacing back and forth in the dugout: now he's out on the field, squaring off with the umpire with whom he disagrees. For males an oblique-angle position is unconsciously perceived as more open and friendly. In his squared-off position, you can bet the baseball manager is not feeling particularly friendly toward the umpire.

Women, on the other hand, are comfortable facing one another more directly.

A friendly oblique orientation for men

Women tend to orient toward each other more directly.

TRY THIS

When approaching a male colleague (regardless of whether you are male or female), do so from the side. When approaching a female, walk directly up to her.

Mirroring

My husband and his father were talking in the kitchen when I walked into the room. I'll always remember that sight: They were sitting at the table, mirror images of each other. Both men were leaning back with their hands behind their heads and their elbows wide apart, and both had their legs loosely crossed. They were deeply engrossed in conversation—totally oblivious to the physical postures they had assumed. I didn't have to overhear what they were saying to realize that (at that moment) father and son were in total rapport.

It's called *limbic synchrony,* and it's hardwired in the human brain.

We all do it. Babies do it even before birth, where their heartbeats and bodily functions have a rhythm that matches those of their mothers. As adults we do it when we are talking with someone we like or are interested in. We subconsciously switch our body posture to match that of the other person— mirroring that person's nonverbal behavior and signaling that we are connected and engaged.

When a colleague mirrors your body language, it's his way of nonverbally saying that he likes or agrees with you. And if you are one of two equal-status executives in a discussion, you may both, unknowingly, be adopting similar postures to maintain your respective positions of authority.

When done with intent, mirroring can be an important part of developing business relationships. Whether you are a team leader, a teacher, or a therapist, an effective way to build rapport (or to increase a person's comfort when he or she is resistant) is to utilize this technique. Mirroring starts by observing a person's body posture and then subtly letting your body reflect his position. If *his* arms are crossed, slowly begin to cross *your* arms. If he leans back, you do the same. In my work as a therapist, I would even mimic a client's breathing pattern—inhaling and exhaling in sync with his or her rhythm.

It's a proven method. A recent research study observed two different teachers as they taught students. One used mirroring; the other did not. The students' reactions were substantially more positive toward the teacher who used mirroring techniques. They believed that that teacher was much more successful, friendly, and appealing.

When a person is closed off or resistant, the easiest way to increase her comfort level is to use mirroring. This technique is useful with clients, sales prospects, customers, and co-workers. It is a silent signal that you are positively relating to the other person. But before you try it out on the boss, you can practice on strangers.

TRY THIS

The next time you are sitting in a waiting room or on an airplane, slowly begin to mirror a person sitting next to you. (This also works in restaurants when the other person is at a different table but there is a line of sight between you.) Subtly mimic the position of his legs and then the movement of arms and hands. Finally, if you are sitting close enough, see if you can inhale and exhale with the same rhythm as the person you are mirroring. You may be surprised at how quickly he responds and starts a conversation with you. (This is *not* the technique to practice on an airplane if you prefer flying without chatting with your seatmate.)

In business situations, you know that you have developed mutual rapport if your partner begins to mirror you in return. Change your arm position and see if she will match your movement into the new posture. If you were to use this technique in a sales presentation and your prospect subconsciously matched your body language, it would be a signal of trust and rapport. But if your prospect mismatched, you should consider the possibility that she isn't yet convinced.

There are other forms of behavioral congruence in which people imitate each other without realizing it. *Interactional synchronizing* occurs when people move at the same time in the same way, simultaneously picking up coffee cups or starting to speak at the same time. This often happens when we are getting along well with another person, and it can feel as though we are on the same wavelength. In fact, synchronizing is the result of our subliminal monitoring of, and responding to, one another's nonverbal cues.

One executive told me that in a negotiation session he often mirrors the posture of the person with whom he's dealing. He noticed that doing so gives him a better sense of

We naturally mirror when we're in rapport.

what the other person is experiencing. I've noticed this as well. Our bodies and emotions are so closely linked that by assuming another person's posture, you are not only gaining rapport but are actually able to get a feel for his or her frame of mind.

In his book *On Becoming a Person: A Therapist's View of Psychotherapy*, psychologist Carl Rogers wrote, "Real communication occurs when we listen with understanding—to see the idea and attitude from the other person's point of view, to sense how it feels to them, to achieve their frame of reference in regard to the thing they are talking about."

Reaching that goal of *real communication*—of understanding, of empathy—is why nonverbal literacy is so crucial to our professional success.

For leaders those communication skills can play a key role in making sure that the workforce truly receives and understands the messages they wish to send. Consider the case of one Fortune 25 company, where "town hall meetings" provided an ongoing opportunity for small groups of employees to get up close and personal with the CEO. Time after time employees would ask about policies or pending organizational changes that had already been communicated in company publications and through dozens of e-mail announcements.

After the meetings the CEO would ask his communications manager, "How many times have we told them about that? Why don't they *know* that?"

"Oh, they know it," the communications manager would reply. "They just want to hear it from you. More importantly, they want to be able to *look* at you when you say it."

The Eyes Have It

THE EYES HAVE BEEN DESCRIBED as the gateway to the soul. They "speak" in the most revealing and accurate language because of the vast amount of information they convey about internal processes.

You may not have thought about it, but we give and receive more messages from the eyes than from any other part of the body. Hostility, anger, affection, welcome, accessibility, amusement, reserve, suspicion, embarrassment, boredom—all can be conveyed by a single glance. This chapter shows why developing the right amount of eye contact is a key professional skill. You'll also learn how pupil size lets you know if you have someone's interest, how to track someone's thinking process by watching his eye movements, how to tell the difference between a business gaze and a social gaze, and why people close their eyes when presented with bad news.

Daniel was well qualified (overqualified, in fact) for the job he was seeking, so when he didn't get hired he was shocked. But when Daniel called the recruiter who sent him out, he was told, "You were fabulous in all the technical aspects, but you freaked out the interviewer because you couldn't look her in the eye."

Whether it's shifty-eyed guilt or wide-eyed innocence, we instinctively link eye gestures to a person's underlying motives. We've heard and used phrases like these all our lives:

"He gave an icy stare."

"She gave him the evil eye."

"If looks could kill..."

"I went in with my eyes wide open."

"He had a gleam in his eye."

"She looked daggers at the other woman."

"He looked down his nose at us."

"We see eye to eye about this."

The Power of Eye Contact

Eye contact is so powerful because it is instinctive and connected with humans' early survival patterns. Children who could attract and maintain eye contact, and therefore increase attention, had the best chance of being fed and cared for. As adults we still put a lot of credence in the signals we give and get from one another's eyes. When people don't look directly at us (so that we can read those important signals) they may, indeed, freak us out!

"I read someplace that eye contact
is a very important business skill."

Eye contact is most effective when both parties feel that its intensity is appropriate for the situation (and this may differ with introverts/extroverts, men/women, or between different cultures). But greater eye contact, especially in intervals lasting four to five seconds, almost always leads to greater liking. So long as someone is looking at us, we believe we have his interest. And if he meets our gaze more than two-thirds of the time, we sense that he finds us appealing or fascinating.

TRY THIS

Here's a short exercise for increasing eye contact: For one day make a mental note of the eye color of everyone you meet. You don't have to remember the color, just notice it. With this one simple exercise, you will dramatically increase your skill at building rapport.

Breaking Eye Contact

It's happened to all of us. You're at a business event, and the person you've been having an intense conversation with begins to shift her gaze from your face to look around the room. Ever wonder why that makes you feel so excluded—as though the person has stopped listening to you? You know it's not logical. She doesn't have to look at you to hear you. People don't listen with their eyes.

Or do they?

Over the course of a conversation, eye contact is made through a series of glances—by the speaker, to make sure the other person has understood or to gage reactions, and by the listener, to indicate interest in either the other person or what's being said. It is also used as a synchronizing signal. A person tends to look up at the end of utterances, which gives the listener warning that the speaker is about to stop

She has stopped listening.

talking. There is often mutual eye contact during attempted interruptions, laughing, and when answering short questions.

In more-intense or more-intimate conversations, people naturally look at one another more often and hold that gaze for longer periods. A sure sign that a conversation is lagging is when one of the participants begins looking away to pay more attention to other people or objects in the vicinity. And when she glances at her watch, gazes blankly into the distance, or visually scans the room, she is giving definite signals with her eyes that she has, in effect, stopped listening.

Eye Contact Avoidance

In most cases too little eye contact is interpreted as being impolite, insincere, or even dishonest. One hospital, analyzing letters from patients, reported that 90 percent of the complaints had to do with doctors' poor eye contact, which was perceived as a lack of caring.

Liars tend to avoid eye contact unless they are very brazen or well rehearsed—in which case liars may actually overcompensate (to "prove" that they are not lying) by making too much eye contact and holding it too long. With this exception the tendency is for people to avoid direct eye contact when lying and, conversely, look with full focus when telling the truth or feeling offended by a false accusation. When people are dishonest or holding back information, they typically meet our gaze less than one-third of the time.

But people also decrease or avoid eye contact when they are discussing something intimate or difficult, when they are not interested in the other person's reactions, when they don't like the other person, when they are insecure or shy (as Daniel was in the interview situation), and when they are ashamed, embarrassed, depressed, or sad.

Waiters in restaurants tend to avoid eye contact with customers when they need to send the message "I'm too busy to deal with you right now." Employees avoid eye contact when the boss poses a difficult question. (The general rule is to look down and shuffle through notes as if searching for the answer.) And when pedestrians or drivers want to ensure their own right of way, one strategy is to avoid meeting the other's eyes to avoid cooperation.

Negative Eye Contact: Staring

Staring is a bold and direct gaze that is continuous, and it's the one example of increased eye contact that does *not* increase liking. In fact, most of us consider staring to be rude or even threatening. This kind of overdone eye contact generally communicates a desire to dominate, a feeling of superiority, a lack of respect, or a wish to insult. During a conversation, when someone challenges what we are saying, she may hold our gaze for longer periods of time, but her eye contact will feel "hard" and her pupils will be constricted.

Darting Eyes

Darting eyes have been linked with deceit so often that it's almost become a cliché. But if you see this eye gesture from someone, keep an open mind about the motive behind it. While darting eyes reliably signal the presence of heightened emotion, that emotion may or may not mean that someone is lying. When people are defensive or insecure about what is happening, their eyes tend to shift from side to side. It's as though they are unconsciously searching for possible escape routes.

Nervousness or anxiety can manifest as darting eyes. And there are many reasons why a person could be nervous. To understand what the behavior means, you still have to interpret the emotion.

Wide Eyes

Wide eyes signal approval and pleased surprise. When someone's eyes open wide in pleasure, her eyebrows rise and her mouth opens slightly. You'll see a subtler version of this expression when someone is discussing something or someone she likes very much.

On the other hand, when people are terrified or enraged, you also see an involuntary, dramatic widening of their eyes. Nicknamed "flashbulb eyes," this gesture is triggered by impulses from the nervous system's fight-or-flight response. In angry individuals flashbulb eyes can be a danger sign of imminent verbal aggression or physical attack.

Pupil Size

Tests with expert card players showed that they won fewer games when their opponents wore dark glasses. Why do you suppose that was? What information was hidden that lowered the experts' chances of success? It seems that they were unconsciously reading their opponents' pupil dilations, and when those opponents wore dark glasses, it knocked out that channel of communication.

Many physical stimuli can cause human pupils to dilate: lighting conditions, some drugs, and even physical exertion. But the most fascinating reason for dilation isn't physical but emotional. Clinical studies by Eckhard Hess, PhD, the former head of the Department of Psychology at the University of Chicago, have shown that the pupil unconsciously widens when the eye sees something pleasant, exciting, or arousing. If people are highly interested or emotionally aroused by what they see, their pupils open to allow them to see more. So when card players saw their opponents' rapid pupil dilation (four aces!), they had "a gut feeling" not to bet on the next hand.

But it's not just card sharks who rely on pupil size for information. We all detect dilation/contraction and respond to those cues. Lovers look deeply into each other's eyes, instinctively looking for pupil dilation that confirms their mutual attraction. Successful salespeople unconsciously monitor pupil dilation (indicating the customer is interested and ready to buy) and pupil contraction (signaling resistance, anger, or negativity).

We are genetically programmed to be influenced by the size of eye pupils. This makes sense, as it would have been

Which do you find more appealing?

highly advantageous for the survival of early humans to know whom to avoid (those who were hostile us) and whom to connect with (those whose interest we aroused). And this programming is just as powerful today. We automatically like people with dilated pupils better than those with contracted pupils.

Studies have shown that people, especially females, are judged to be more attractive if their pupils are wide open and more dilated than normal. To increase the appeal of any product that uses full-face pictures in its ads, just alter the image and make the pupil size larger. Using this technique Barbara Pease and Alan Pease, authors of *The Definitive Book of Body Language,* helped increase the direct catalog sales for Revlon lipsticks by 45 percent!

The ability to decode pupil dilation is also hardwired into the brain, and it happens automatically but unconsciously. (The expert card players thought they were reacting to their intuition.) Because a person's pupil changes are not under his control, they provide a very reliable indication of interest, attraction, and emotional attitude. Once you start paying close attention, you'll find that pupils have a lot to teach you.

By the way, outside of using eye drops (which I don't recommend) there's not much you can do to artificially dilate your pupils. It can be useful to remember that pupils dilate automatically in low-light conditions. This may explain why everyone looks interested in everyone else they encounter in a dimly lit bar!

The Mind's Eye

Years ago when I was a therapist, I studied Neuro-Linguistic Programming and learned to track what people were thinking by watching their eye movements. When people think, they access different parts of the brain depending on the information being sought—and their eyes reveal clues to that process.

Most right-handed people, when thinking about something they've seen, let their eyes defocus or look up and to the left. (These eye signals are reversed for most left-handed people.) If someone were describing her apartment or house, her eyes move to this direction. When right-handers are *creating* an image (as they would if instructed to think of a "purple cow"), their eyes generally look up and to the right. If they are recalling something they've heard (their mother's voice or a school bell, for example), they look to the left and tilt their head as though listening. If they are remembering a

Recalling an image

Creating an image

Remembering sound, music, and voices

Accessing emotion or sensation   *Talking to herself*

feeling (either a physical sensation or an emotion), they look down and to the right. People talking silently to themselves also look down but to the left.

TRY THIS

Test this out on a couple of colleagues. Ask them this series of questions and watch their eyes as they reply. If they are right-handed, their eye movements should look like this:

▶ What was the color of your first automobile? (up and to the left)

▶ What would a rainbow look like if the colors were backward? (up and to the right)

▶ What is the most distinct sound you can remember from your childhood? (sideways toward an ear)

▶ How does it feel to relax on a warm, sandy beach? (down and to the right)

▶ Can you recite the words to your favorite song silently to yourself? (down and to the left)

Catching all these fleeting eye signals takes practice, but by simply observing more closely you will know whether someone most typically thinks in pictures, words, or feelings. Remember, though, not *all* right-handed people display these same patterns. The trick is to get to know an individual's eye cues so that you interpret them accurately. With this knowledge you can (as I did in my counseling practice) literally speak their language: *"Look* at it from this perspective," "Does this *sound* good to you?" or "What do you *feel* is the right thing to do?" You'll also have a glimpse into whether someone is recalling something she's actually seen (eyes up and to the left) or if she is visualizing an imagined or made-up scene (eyes up and to the right).

Business Gaze and Social Gaze

An attractive manager was having problems dealing with the male employees in her department. "They never take me seriously," she complained. "It's as though they think I'm flirting with them. Which I definitely am not!"

After watching her interact with members of her staff, I saw the problem. She was trying to discuss work-related issues while using a social gaze.

Here's what I mean: If you create an imaginary triangle, with the eyes at the base and the apex at midforehead, you have mapped out the "look of business"—the *business gaze.* When you keep your gaze in that area, you nonverbally signal a no-nonsense, businesslike approach.

When you invert the triangle and move your focus from the eyes to the mouth, you turn your gaze into one more appropriate for social encounters. And a *social gaze* can be misinterpreted as flirtatious—even in a business setting.

Business gaze area   *Social gaze area*

It's also interesting to note that in group dynamics the person whose eye level is highest is usually perceived as the leader. Watch what happens as new people join the group, and you'll see newcomers turn to address that person first.

TRY THIS

Test this for yourself. In some professional conversations, keep your gaze focused in the business area triangle. In others lower your gaze to the social area. Notice how that one small gaze shift can create different responses in the people you are addressing.

Knowledge about the business gaze doesn't mean that you should never look in someone's social area triangle. It can be highly effective to do so—using direct eye contact only when you want to emphasize important points. But women, especially, need to be aware that to be taken seriously in business interactions, a business gaze has the most impact.

Blinking Rates

During conversation a normal blink rate is six to eight blinks per minute—and the eyelids are closed for about one-tenth of a second. This rate speeds up when someone is under pressure. For example, when most people are lying, their blinking rate increases dramatically. Police interrogators and customs inspectors look for a change in the blink rate that might signify areas where the person is trying to cover something up. Psychologists are also aware of the significance of the blink rate when a patient is trying to conceal something. Of course, rapid blinking can also indicate annoying lighting in the room or a heightened level of anxiety for a variety of reasons. It could even be exhibited if a person is telling the truth but is worried or insecure about not being believed.

Elongated Blinking

Elongated blinking is an unconscious gesture other people use to exclude you during a conversation. When someone's eyelids close for more than a second, it is an attempt to block you from their sight. And when combined with a backward head tilt (a looking-down-the-nose gesture), it's also a sign that the person is bored with you, is completely disinterested in the topic, or feels superior.

He's displaying a smug sense of superiority.

Eye Roll

This is the classic eye movement of a teenager listening to advice from a parent. Whenever you see people rolling their eyes, you know they are highly skeptical or simply don't believe whatever you just said.

Sideways Glance

A sideways glance can indicate interest or hostility, depending on what other facial gestures accompany it. When combined with raised eyebrows or a smile, you can assume that the person is sending a signal of interest or flirtation. Down-turned eyebrows and a down-turned mouth, however, signal suspicion, hostility, or criticism.

Lowered Gaze

One nonverbal sign of submission is a lowered gaze. If it is accompanied with a slight lowering of the head (or a bow, such as is prevalent in Japanese culture), it signals an even greater respectful or submissive attitude.

Lowered Head, Looking Up

A gesture that is really a cluster of nonverbal behaviors is lowering the head with a tilt to one side while looking up. This submissive gesture, displayed primarily by females, mimics the upward gaze of little children. For that reason it almost always touches a parental instinct in both men and women.

Princess Diana was often photographed using this gesture—an unconscious bid for public sympathy and support.

This gesture earned Princess Diana the nickname Shy Di.

Eye Blocks

A sales manager had bad news to deliver. The company was merging with another organization and consolidating sales forces, with the result that most of her staff was considered "redundant." I watched as she made this announcement, and I noticed that people closed their eyes for a few moments on hearing the unwelcome news.

Our eyes are more remarkable than any camera, and they have evolved as the primary way we get information about the world around us. But eyes that invite input can also block it. In fact, *eye blocking* is a survival mechanism that evolved to protect the brain from seeing undesirable or threatening images. Eye blocks include closing eyes, rubbing eyes, and covering eyes with hands or objects. Eye blocking takes place so frequently that most people miss it completely or ignore its very significant meaning.

TRY THIS

If you are making an announcement and you want to know someone's gut-level reaction to it, follow the eyes. You'll notice that people's eyes travel to good news and flee from bad news. And if people block or close their eyes, it's a good bet that they are feeling threatened or saddened by what they've heard.

Tearing Eyes

It was an emotional awards ceremony. The company had just gone through a very challenging time, and the CEO was acknowledging those past difficulties while thanking employees who had pulled together to bring the company back from the brink of bankruptcy. As the CEO went on to pay tribute to select individuals for going far beyond the call of duty, his eyes filled with tears and he had to leave the stage for a few moments. He was simply overwhelmed by his feelings—and everyone in the audience understood that.

At the most elementary level, tearing is a physical response to allergies, foreign particles in the eye, fumes (like ammonia or onions), and pain or injury. But eye moisture and tears are so much more. They often say what can't be adequately expressed with words.

Tears evolved as a way to increase attachment bonds between infants and parents. They remain a compelling trigger—again, embedded in our hardwiring—that commands a response from others of compassion, attention, understanding, or sympathy. Tears can be faked by professional actors or talented amateurs, but when tears are genuine (as they were with the CEO) they are an eloquent statement that something intensely emotional is taking place.

"Please talk to me, Michael.
Something's bothering you, isn't it?"

So we've got the eyes covered. Make that *un*covered. Compelling, rejecting, concealing, revealing—whatever signal they send, the eyes do, indeed, *have* it, which is why you're now ready to take a fresh new look—literally—at the people with whom you do business. You'll be surprised at how often the body language of the eyes reveals new insights and new meanings in your professional interactions with others.

CHAPTER 4

Face to Face

RESEARCH SHOWS that reading facial expressions is a latent ability within all of us—never lost, merely neglected. Human beings can send and receive facial signals with lightning speed and over great distances. We can tell in a blink if a stranger's face is registering surprise or pleasure, even if he or she is 150 feet away.

This chapter is your opportunity to reconnect with that innate talent and turn it into a professional skill. You'll discover the six facial expressions common to human beings around the world, learn how to tell a real smile from a fake one, and understand why people are susceptible to emotional contagion. You'll also learn how to decode a variety of signals sent by facial features and head positions. Just imagine how much more effectively you will deal with co-workers or customers when you know what you are really seeing when you look them in the face!

We communicate with facial gestures and head movements a lot more than we realize, and someone trained in reading them can have a big advantage. But here's the thing about all nonverbal cues: you may read them accurately but still misinterpret the motive behind the behavior.

Consider a situation that faced Bob, who works in a district attorney's office and often sits next to the DA during trials. Bob has become adept at reading the body language of jurors, using that knowledge to figure out which jury members are in sync with the state's case and which are going to be tougher to convince.

But even he can be wrong.

At a recent murder trial, the prosecutor was questioning her crime scene analyst as a gory set of slides of the victim were being shown. All the jurors were paying rapt attention to the photos and the investigator's testimony—all the jurors, that is, except one, a macho-looking man who kept turning his head away, as though the photos were unimportant. "That's the guy we're going to have trouble with," Bob predicted. "He's obviously not interested in our evidence." But at the end of the trial, the verdict was unanimous: guilty.

I'll say it again: you may accurately pick up nonverbal cues but still misinterpret the motive behind them. That's what happened to Bob. He was right on target about the juror's blank stare, head turn, and avoidance of the photos. But what Bob took for disinterest was really queasiness. When Bob interviewed the juror after the trial, he found out that this big, burly man couldn't bear to look at the gruesome crime scene photos.

So, keep this in mind as you practice your ability to read facial expressions: they do not reveal what is generating a particular emotion, only that the emotion is occurring. Even as you increase your accuracy in picking up nonverbal signals (and you'll be a lot better off being aware of these cues than oblivious to them), you will always have to dig a little to uncover the exact motivation behind the expression.

TRY THIS

For a full day, pay attention to different emotions that are being expressed by your co-workers or clients. As soon as you see one, write it down. Now here's the hard part: just write the emotion you detect, *not* the cause: "She looks sad," not "She's disappointed with the presentation." "He looks fearful," not "He's afraid we'll lose the account." "The boss looks angry," not "The boss is mad at me for coming late to the meeting."

Omitting the suspected motivation is difficult to do because we all have a tendency to jump to conclusions about the causes behind expressions. I'm not saying that your assumptions about causes are wrong, just that they *may* be. And this gives you a chance to stop, observe, and then explore alternatives.

Universal Expressions

A longstanding debate involved the origins of various facial expressions. On one side of the argument was Charles Darwin, who had written in 1872 about the consistency of expressions in mammals. On the opposing side were prominent social scientists of the 1960s and 1970s—including anthropologist Margaret Mead—who believed that facial expressions are learned through culture. So, who was right? Are facial expressions innate or are they culturally influenced?

The issue was settled by Paul Ekman, PhD, a professor of psychology at the University of California at San Francisco (UCSF). His research proved that there are six expressions that are universally recognized and understood: joy, sadness, surprise, fear, contempt/disgust, and anger.

So much for culture! From the jungles of Papua New Guinea to the jam-packed streets of New York City, wherever you go in the world, everyone shares and recognizes these facial gestures—and relates to the emotions they portray. Because this musculature is directly connected to the areas of the brain that process emotion, very few people are able to consciously control all their facial expressions.

Another finding of Dr. Ekman and his research team at UCSF was how fleeting facial expressions—called *microexpressions*—often allow the truth to slip through in brief, unguarded moments. Lasting less than one-fifth of a second, these flashes of expression are glimpses of a person's true emotional state. We *don't* think before we feel. Initial-reaction expressions tend to show up on the face before we're even conscious of experiencing an emotion.

Reading faces is not just a matter of identifying static expressions but also of noticing how faces subtly begin to change. People in face-to-face exchanges watch each other's expressions to gauge reactions to what's being said and heard. Even when some words are missed, observing the expression on a speaker's face can help the listener follow a conversation.

Because each emotion has unique, identifiable signals, the face is the only system that tells us the specific emotion that's occurring. Currently, the federal government is funding two major computer teams—one at the University of Pittsburgh and one at University of California at San Diego—that are trying to automate the Facial Action Coding System developed by Paul Ekman, Wallace V. Friesen, and Joseph C. Hager. It is predicted that within a few years an automatic system will enable computers to produce a readout of changes in your emotional state, moment by moment.

Examples of Universal Expressions

Joy Intense and exultant happiness is depicted by smiling, raised cheeks, dimples, and eyes crinkled at the corners.

Sadness A forehead wrinkled with grief, inner eyebrows raised, and down-turned corners of the mouth indicate sorrow and unhappiness.

Surprise Wonder, astonishment, or amazement, as at something unanticipated, is depicted by raised eyebrows, eyes open wide, and the lower jaw often dropped, allowing the lips to part. Surprise is the most fleeting of facial expressions; it may flicker across the face in less than a second.

Fear Eyebrows raised and drawn together, eyes open wide with the lid tense, and lips stretched back indicate a feeling of agitation and anxiety caused by the presence or imminence of danger.

 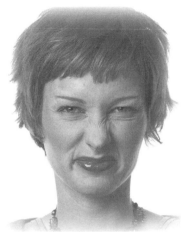

Disgust/contempt Aversion or repugnance is conveyed with a wrinkled nose, lowered eyebrows, a raised upper lip, and the eyes squeezed almost completely shut. This expression, which originated with foul tastes and smells, has also become the body language of contempt we reserve for foul people and actions.

Anger Rage or hostility are evident in eyebrows that are drawn together and lowered, an intense gaze with both the upper and lower eyelids tense and narrowed, and the lips tightly pressed together.

TRY THIS

Watch a TV show or a movie with the sound turned off—daytime soap operas work very well for this. Focus on the characters' facial expressions and guess what their emotional relationship to one another is. The good thing about soaps is that if you tune in the next day, you'll see almost the same scenes with the accompanying dialogue, so you can assess your accuracy.

Fake Expressions

One way to tell if an expression is genuine is to notice if it is symmetrical. Fake or forced expressions often create an "unmatched face," whereby the same expression appears on both sides of the face but is more pronounced on one side.

Another element in catching a fake expression is timing. According to Dr. Ekman's studies, expressions that last a long time—between five and ten seconds—are probably false. An expression of true emotion is much shorter. For example, an expression of genuine surprise is a fleeting event, taking place in less than a second.

And watch someone's timing. If an expression of anger comes after angry words, it is probably fabricated. Usually, a genuine display of emotion comes before or with the verbal message.

Emotional Contagion

It started out to be a wonderful day. The sun was shining, and I was singing along with my favorite radio station while driving through unusually light traffic to the San Francisco airport. Then, as I was turning into the airport parking lot, a driver abruptly pulled in front of me and glared in his rearview mirror. At the ticket counter, the employee frowned and sighed as I explained the need to make changes to my itinerary. By the time a scowling flight attendant took my ticket, I scowled right back. My good mood had been contaminated!

No one is immune to emotional contagion. Facial gestures and their underlying emotions (both positive and negative) are highly infectious, and "catching" them is a universal human phenomenon. We all tend to mimic the facial expressions and reflect the moods of those with whom we have contact. Getting a genuine smile can brighten up our day, and angry frowns are upsetting.

We're hardwired to mimic expressions and emotions and have been doing so since infancy. Nine-month-old babies look longer at their mothers and express greater joy when their mothers are themselves joyful. One-year-olds, after watching a videotape of an actress portraying either positive or negative feelings, mimic the actress's expressions and alter their own emotions accordingly.

"The waiters here are so darn cheerful."

As adults we remain susceptible. Swedish researchers found that merely seeing a picture of a happy face produces fleeting activity in the muscles that pull the mouth into a smile. In fact, whenever we look at a photograph of someone portraying any strong emotion, such as sadness, disgust, or joy, our facial muscles automatically start to mirror that expression. And it isn't just a physical response because our expressions subtly trigger the corresponding feelings.

TRY THIS

Each of us gives and responds to hundreds of facial expressions daily—from co-workers' grins to clenched-jaw displays around the conference table. Looked at another way, you are part of an emotional chain-reaction effect in your personal and professional lives.

For one full day, make a conscious choice to spread only positive emotions. As you go through the day, notice how other people's negative emotions may try to contaminate your good mood. The trick is to not let them do so. Instead, simply acknowledge what is happening, regroup, and get back on track!

Group Feelings

A business simulation experiment at Yale University assigned two groups of people the task of deciding how much of a bonus to give each employee from a set fund. Each person in the group was to get as large a bonus as possible for certain employees while being fair to the entire employee population.

In one group the conflicting agendas led to stress and tension, while in the second group everyone ended up feeling good about the result. The difference was in the "plants"— actors who had been secretly assigned to each group. In the first group, the actor was negative and downbeat and, in the second group, positive and upbeat. The emotional tone of the meetings followed the lead of each actor—although none of the group members understood why his or her feelings had shifted.

In my change-management consulting, I've noticed that in times of organizational uncertainty employees instinctively pay more attention to the facial expressions of those around them. People search for smiles or frowns to get a better sense of how to interpret and react to a situation, and then they mimic the predominant emotions.

TRY THIS

The next time your boss tries to convince you that "this change is for the best" but you and your colleagues aren't buying it, see if you can figure out why. Are the boss's facial expressions or body language out of sync with what she's saying? Is there some influential person in the room whose negative facial expression (and its emotional undertone) is being picked up by the rest of the group?

Messages from the Face: Forehead to Chin

Furrowed brow Concentration or puzzlement may be shown in the forehead as the eyebrows come together while the person considers alternatives or ponders what he or she just read or heard.

Eyebrow flash The rapid raising of the inside corners of the eyebrows—the *eyebrow flash*—is common to every culture. This involuntary signal of recognition and interest has been observed among Europeans, Balinese, Bushmen, and South American Indians. In fact, the eyebrow flash appears to be used by virtually every society and social grouping, from Afghan tribesmen to New York stockbrokers. (The only people known to suppress this facial gesture are the Japanese. They are perfectly capable of exchanging such a signal, but it is considered improper.)

TRY THIS

Try catching the eye of a total stranger and quickly raising both eyebrows. You'll find that most people will either greet you verbally or respond with an eyebrow lift of their own.

Other Eyebrow Signals

If someone is annoyed, his facial muscles draw the eyebrows down and toward the center of the face. Lowering the eyebrows is how humans show dominance or aggression toward others.

Raising the eyebrows may be a sign of submission or a request for approval. When someone is unsure about whether he is believed or how an action is accepted, you commonly see the eyebrows raise and pause—even if just momentarily. This is an unspoken inquiry: "Did I get it right?" "What do you think of what I just said?"

The gesture of raising the eyebrows slowly, over a few seconds, along with a tilted head usually comes at the end of a sentence as a nonverbal inquiry to see if the listener has understood. And when the movement occurs even more slowly, with a lift of the head, it can signal disapproval. Raising one eyebrow, especially if accompanied by a slight smirk, shows skepticism. But the ultimate dismissive signal is when the eyebrows lift, the lips purse, and the head lowers and turns slightly away.

The Nose Knows

When people prepare for a physical action, they take a deep breath, which causes the nostrils to expand. This *nose flare* is a good indicator that someone intends to do something physical. An agent with the Federal Bureau of Investigation (FBI) said, "If I see a suspect looking down [an act of conceal-ment] and his nose is flaring, there's a high probability he's preparing to take a swing at me."

Although you most likely don't have anyone prepar-ing to punch you at a business meeting, a nose flare in this environment becomes a signal of intention or engagement. It is giving you advance warning that the person is about to make a statement or take some other action. A nose crinkle from someone at the same meeting probably means that she thinks there's something fishy about what was just said.

Something doesn't smell right to her.

Blushing Cheeks

No other part of the body reacts more dramatically to a flow of blood than the cheeks. This telltale sign is a simple physiological fact. When you are emotionally aroused—whether angry or excited—blood rushes to the face in various degrees. And when a person is nervous or embarrassed, he blushes.

Taut Skin

Tenseness and anger can be detected by looking for tightness around the cheeks, along the jaw line, and in the neck. To get a feel for this, try holding your breath and feel the increased stiffness in these areas on yourself.

Smiles: Real and Fake

A fake smile is the most common facial expression used to mask other emotions. A person who doesn't want her true feelings revealed (especially if she wants to disguise displeasure or anger) may "put on a happy face."

Dr. Paul Ekman identified eighteen distinct smiles—most of them false. One of the most common in organizational situations is the "qualifier" smile, which bosses use when rejecting an idea or criticizing an employee. And we all use the fake smile in business settings when we don't really feel an emotional closeness to those around us; the real smile is reserved for those we truly care about.

We've had a lot of practice doing this. We've been displaying both real and fake smiles all our lives. According to studies at the University of Maryland, ten-month-old infants curve their lips in response to the coo of friendly strangers, but they produce happy, genuine smiles only at the approach of their mothers.

A fake smile is easy to produce: it takes only one set of muscles to stretch the lip corners sideways and create a grin. But a false smile is also easy to detect. A genuine smile not

Genuine smile　　　　　　　**Smile that doesn't
reach the eyes**

only affects the corners of the mouth but changes the entire face: the eyes light up, the forehead wrinkles, the cheek muscles rise, skin around the eyes and the mouth crinkles, and finally the mouth turns up.

Another signal of a genuine smile (and one that is almost impossible to fake) is a lowering of the inner corner of the eyebrows. The absence of lowered eyebrows is one reason why false smiles look so strained and stiff.

Real smiles are also difficult to fake when we feel negative emotions. The polite smile offered by a bored salesclerk, or by someone hearing a joke for the hundredth time, pulls up the lips but, literally, stops there.

If you look at a photo of someone smiling and cover their lips, their eyes reveal everything about their real feelings. Mo Williams, an illustrator and author of children's books, says that if he draws a face with unhappy eyes and a smiling mouth, it is a picture of a sad face. So there you have it! The truth of a smile is in (and around) the eyes.

Whatever their origin or motivation, smiles have a powerful effect on all of us. The human brain prefers happy faces, recognizing them more quickly than those with negative expressions. Smiles are such an important part of communication that we spot a smile at 300 feet—the length of a football field. And if you ever go to trial, keep this in mind: although courtroom judges are equally likely to find smilers and nonsmilers guilty, they tend to give smilers lighter penalties, a phenomenon called the *smile-leniency effect.*

*"I'd really like to take another look at
Dr. Odett's happy-face theory."*

Reading Lips

Mouth movements can give away all sorts of emotional clues. When people are nervous, their mouths become dry, so lip touching or licking becomes a pacifying behavior to cope with anxiety or concern. Biting the lower lip is also an indicator of stress, often seen when people are trying to hold back a comment.

Pursed lips (sometimes twisted to the side) are a common gesture when thinking over options. Pursing one's lips can also be a signal that the person is in disagreement with someone or something. This is often seen in court trials. While one attorney speaks, opposing counsel purses her lips in disagreement. Judges also do it as they disagree with attorneys at sidebar conferences.

Pressing lips tightly together occurs when someone is angry, frustrated, dismayed, or trying to hold back information. Tight lips are almost always associated with

She's considering her options.

He's holding something back.

**He doesn't like it, but
he's resigned to it.**

negative emotions. That is one of the reasons why full lips
are so appealing—they are subconsciously interpreted as a
signal that people are responding to us in a positive way.

Lips that form as if to blow out air are almost always associated with resignation, skepticism, or frustration.

A completely involuntary move that a mouth makes is to
quiver as a result of being startled. That's exactly what happened when I saw a grocery clerk accidentally knock over
a display in the store—and her shaking lower lip and chin
registered her surprise and dismay.

Yawning

Usually, when we see someone yawning we think they are
bored or tired. But psychologists now believe that yawning may be an escape mechanism used to avoid difficult
or stressful issues. People may yawn rather than discuss a
painful subject.

Bored, tired, or just doesn't want to talk about it?

I once coached an executive whose son had a behavioral problem. This woman could successfully lead an international organization, but she couldn't control her child. I began to notice that whenever we discussed the trouble her son was having—and especially when we talked about her role as a mother—she would inevitably let out a yawn. It was her way of trying to avoid the whole subject.

Tongue Flick

People stick out their tongues to lick their lips when under stress or when thinking about a delicious meal. But there is another gesture, where the tongue juts from between the teeth *without* touching the lips. It happens very quickly and reminds me of a snake flicking its tongue. And this gesture is almost always a signal of deception.

I was in an automobile repair shop, and the mechanic had just quoted me the "best possible price" to fix my car. He then left the area to get a final okay from his manager. They were behind a glass partition, so I couldn't hear their conversation, but I could see everything their bodies were saying. And what I saw was my mechanic giving a quick but unmistakable tongue flick as he finished talking with his boss.

Obviously, a tongue flick is a totally unconscious gesture; so if you are ever negotiating with someone who displays it, you can be assured that he's making it clear (without knowing it) that he thinks he is getting away with something.

When the mechanic returned, he assured me that his manager agreed it was the best price they were able to offer. I declined his service and subsequently found a repair shop that fixed the problem at half the cost.

Chin Jut

Someone who is angry or defensive tends to jut the chin forward. You can see chin jutting in small children who don't want to do something. Right before they holler, "No!" they'll stick their chins out. Your colleagues may display a similar behavior when they are getting angry, feel they have been wronged, or are about to tell someone off.

He's mad!

Swallowing

Swallowing is especially conspicuous in males, with the up-and-down motion of the Adam's apple—called the *Adam's apple jump*. This jump is a sign of emotional anxiety, embarrassment, or stress. For example, I've noticed in business meetings that a listener's Adam's apple may inadvertently jump if he dislikes or strongly disagrees with a speaker's suggestion, perspective, or point of view.

Head Positions

Head tilt In primitive tribes, tilting the head was a way of hearing more clearly to be alerted to sounds of danger. Today head tilting is a signal that someone is interested and involved, and it is a particularly feminine gesture. Head tilts can be very positive cues, but they are also subconsciously processed

as submission signals. In business dealings with men, women should keep their heads straight up in a more neutral position—or should at least be aware of the nonverbal message they are sending when they don't.

A feminine gesture that's not very professional

Head shifts When people are uttering or listening to a message that makes them uncomfortable, their heads may shift away from whomever they are talking to. This is an attempt to create distance. Watch for an abrupt jerking back of the head or a slow deliberate withdrawal. Both are signs of discomfort.

Head duck "Look out below!" The posture you'd instinctively assume in reaction to this cry is to raise your shoulders and pull your head down between them. It's the same posture I've seen many employees take as they approach their boss.

He's insecure, and she's the boss.

In a business context, the head duck is a signal that often reveals the status and relationship between individuals.

Head held high Many years ago an experiment was conducted with a group of students who smoked cigarettes. After the results of an exam were given out, the students were observed to see if they had passed or failed the test. Those students who had done well exhaled their cigarette smoke upward, while those who had performed poorly exhaled downward. It's all about head position. Feelings of high confidence unconsciously pull the head up. Feelings of low confidence lower it.

Head nods   Just as shaking the head from side to side is an almost universal gesture meaning "no" or "I don't agree," *head nods*—the up and down movement of the head—are recognized in most cultures as indicators of approval, understanding, or agreement. When someone nods slowly, it usually indicates an ongoing interest in whoever is speaking. Fast nodding signals impatience with the speaker or the listener's desire to get a turn to speak.

In a well-known experiment, a group of psychology students controlled the behavior of their professor: Every time the teacher walked to the left side of the classroom, the students would smile and nod encouragement. When the teacher walked to the right side, the students would look bored and disinterested. By the end of the class, the professor was virtually glued to the left side of the room.

TRY THIS

The next time you are in a conversation where you're trying to encourage the other person to speak more, nod your head using clusters of three nods at regular intervals. Research shows that people talk three to four times more than usual when the listener nods in this fashion. You'll be amazed at how this single nonverbal signal can trigger such a positive response.

The head nod is tremendously important in communication. You say something, and I nod as you say it. That tells you I'm listening and I understand. Then I speak, and you nod that you agree. In public speaking or when addressing a small group, the head nods tell you whether you are connecting with an audience.

Without head nods people may not even want to talk to you. One of my clients wondered why his business conversations so rarely gave him the results he was looking for. After watching him for a few minutes, it was obvious: he would talk and listen without ever moving his head. This so disturbed his co-workers (although they didn't quite know what it was they found so disturbing) that they avoided any conversations with him—and shortened the ones they were forced to have!

Being on the lookout for head nods—and using them yourself—is one of the easier body language signals you can put to work on a regular basis.

Like all the facial and head gestures mentioned in this chapter, you'll find that your increased awareness of the smallest nonverbal cue—a tilt of the head or a pursing of the lips—may have a profound effect on your ability to understand the deeper meaning of signals that people at work are sending you all the time.

CHAPTER 5

Talking with Your Hands

JANE IS TELLING IAN A STORY. At a crucial point, one of her characters slips a lethal substance into somebody else's drink. To illustrate the action, Jane holds her hand in a C shape and tilts it, as if pouring from a cup. Nothing strange about that, you might think, except that Jane is blind and well aware that Ian is, too.

Hand and arm gestures not only are an adjunct to speech but may be our oldest method of communication. Researchers now believe that early humans communicated using a form of mime. Somewhere in our evolutionary history, speech took over from gesture as the main form of communication, but gesture and speech are so tightly connected that we can't do one without the other. It's an old, old habit, and it doesn't die just because we are on the telephone or talking to someone who is blind.

This chapter illustrates how hand and arm gestures have become an integral part of business communication. You'll learn why people who use a variety of gestures are usually judged to be more personable, how emblematic gestures differ from those produced without conscious awareness, and how to decode gestures of low and high levels of confidence and of sincerity, anxiety, deception, evaluation, boredom, and resistance.

Everybody gestures. Sometimes physical movements are used to illustrate a point (like pointing to a paragraph in a contract). Some are used to control another person's speech (putting a hand up like a stop sign), and others are used as a substitute for speech (a motorist displaying irritation at another driver by using a rude finger gesture). But we also produce gestures spontaneously and unwittingly as we speak. We may seldom think of our gestures consciously, but in practice we use them with great efficiency and sophistication to cover a surprisingly wide range of communication.

There's another powerful reason why we use our hands when we speak. Brain imaging has shown that a region called Broca's area, which is important for speech production, is active not only when we're talking but also when we wave our hands. Because gesture is integrally linked to speech, gesturing as we talk might actually power up our thinking. In experiments with nearly a hundred children and adults, researchers found that gesturing—as subjects explained how they had solved a math problem—improved recall of a previously memorized list of numbers or letters. When asked to keep their hands still as they talked, the subjects didn't remember as well.

"Your honor, the witness has his fingers crossed!"

TRY THIS

The next time someone is talking to you, pretend that you didn't quite understand and ask her to repeat something she just said. Watch to see if she adds gestures she hadn't used before. I'll bet she does! People realize on an unconscious level that gestures help clarify and convince.

From the Inside Out

Have you ever noticed that when people are passionate about what they're saying, their gestures become more animated? Their hands and arms move about, emphasizing points and conveying enthusiasm.

You may not have been aware of this connection before, but you instinctively felt it. Research shows that we all tend to view in a more favorable light those people who use a greater variety of gestures. Studies have found that people who communicate through active gesturing tend to be evaluated as "warm, agreeable, and energetic," whereas those who remain still are seen as "logical, cold, and analytical."

When we're enthusiastic, our gestures become animated.

It is also interesting to note the equation of hand and arm movement with energy. If you wanted to project more enthusiasm and drive (say, in an interview), you could do so by increased gesturing. On the other hand, over-gesturing with flailing arms, especially when hands are raised above the shoulders, can make you appear out of control, *less* believable, and *less* powerful.

TRY THIS

Pay attention at the next company party you attend. Most interaction at parties involves individuals who are standing and holding drinks. This limits the number of hand gestures that can be made. If you are listening to someone who is excited about her topic, you'll probably notice her putting down the glass so that she can use her hands for emphasis. But if another conversation is with someone just passing time, she will gesture very little and hardly ever put down her glass.

Another phenomenon to observe in conversations is the *gestural echo.* Watch a group of people talking and note how, when one person uses a specific gesture, others will use it later.

Emblematic Gestures

Some gestures have an agreed-upon meaning to a group and are consciously used instead of words. These are referred to as

"That's *my performance review?! Two thumbs up?!"*

emblematic gestures, and, like the words they represent, they're processed in the left hemisphere of the brain.

We learn emblematic gestures at home, in school, and in other social environments, so they generally differ from culture to culture.

Here are some examples you'll recognize in any North American organization:

- The thumbs-up sign is commonly understood to mean "good job," "okay," or "everything's fine."

A double thumbs-up for a really good job

- Hand rocking—where the palm faces down, the fingers spread out, and the hand rocks left and right—means "so-so" or "maybe."

- The two-fingered V-sign (also used as a "peace sign") communicates a victory.

- A shoulder shrug, especially when accompanied with a palms-up gesture, means the person doesn't know, doesn't understand, or doesn't care.

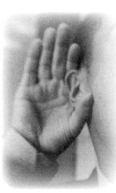

What did you say?

- A hand cupping the ear says, "I can't hear you."

- Slapping the forehead is a way to communicate, "Oh no, I completely forgot!" or "How stupid of me!"

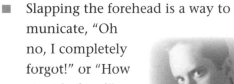

- Holding the thumb straight down means "bad idea" or "no."

A classic sign of rejection

Hand-to-mouth Deception Cues

Unlike emblematic gestures, most hand and arm gestures are not deliberate actions. Instead they are movements that are subconsciously ingrained. Everyone unconsciously gestures to convey messages about how they really feel. And these are the gestures you want to be able to spot and correctly decode when working with people.

Take the *hand-to-mouth deception cue* for example. When young children tell a lie, they usually cover their mouth with one or both hands—as if trying to hold back (too late!) an action they know to be wrong. Older children figure out that this gesture is a dead giveaway that they are being deceitful, so they try to stop it. The problem is that this action has already become habitual and, instead of stopping, it merely transforms into a more subdued and subtle gesture. Deception signals seen in adults include fingers casually covering or touching the mouth (possibly disguised as a fake cough or used to conceal a yawn) or a hand headed for the mouth,

He doesn't believe you.

hesitating at the last moment, and then barely grazing a lip or rubbing the nose instead.

People who are lying may also touch their nose because the rush of adrenaline opens the capillaries and it itches. Watch closely and you'll notice that when someone is about to lie or make an outrageous statement, he'll often unconsciously rub his nose.

People touch their mouth or nose not only when they are lying but also when *listening* to someone they *think* is lying. So when Kim, a police officer, interviews two suspects at the same time, she pays particular attention to the hand-to-mouth gestures of both people.

TRY THIS

The next time you're leading a meeting or giving a business presentation, notice if any audience members cover or block their mouth. If you see this gesture, use it as a signal to stop and address their disbelief: "I know some of you have doubts about what I've just said," or "You look skeptical. Can you tell me what your concerns are?"

Pacifying Gestures

In the course of human development, we as a species developed a repertoire of pacifying behaviors to help our bodies deal with stress. Infants and young children display these behaviors when they suck their thumbs, stroke the silky trim of a blanket, or reach for an aptly named pacifier.

As we grow older, other adaptive behaviors take over.

To soothe themselves, people rub their legs. They pull at their collars. They cross their arms and rub their hands against their upper arms in a kind of self-hug. They place the fingers of one hand in the palm of the other and lightly

***Self-touching
when surprised***

massage the fingertips, thereby creating not only a pacifying action but a physical barrier as well.

Any hand-to-body touching can be calming. Self-touching gestures are particularly telling of shame, doubt, anxiety, and surprise.

Touching is particularly effective in sensitive areas like the face and the neck. Stroking the face, rubbing the forehead, pulling or massaging the earlobe with thumb and forefinger, or playing with the hair can serve as pacifying behaviors. Nervous eating, biting fingernails, or nibbling on a pencil are also "grown-up" manifestations of this early hardwired response to stress.

Touching or rubbing one's neck is one of the most significant and frequent pacifying responses to internal or external stressors. Pulling at a collar can also be an indirect way to get more "breathing room." Be especially aware of someone stroking himself under the chin above the Adam's apple and tugging at the fleshy part of the neck. This area is rich with

He has his doubts.

nerve endings that, when stroked, reduce blood pressure, lower heart rate, and calm the individual down.

Women, by the way, pacify by touching their necks differently than men do. They sometimes touch or twist necklaces they are wearing. They also touch or cover the hollow area right below the Adam's apple—sometimes referred to as the neck dimple—when they feel threatened, fearful, or anxious.

TRY THIS

Stay alert for pacifying gestures. If you are a manager who's just announced a new work schedule and one of your staff members rubs the back of her neck (the pain-in-the-neck gesture), ask her about her concerns. If you are a salesperson and your prospect starts to scratch his head, realize that he may still be unconvinced—so mention product warranties and customer endorsements to reassure him.

The open gestures of candor

Open Palms

When law enforcement officers are trained in interrogation techniques, they are taught that one of the key places to look for honesty is the palms of the hands. It is very difficult for most of us to lie with the palms of our hands exposed. When being truthful or forthcoming, people tend to use open gestures, showing their palms and wrists and spreading hands and arms away from their bodies, as if saying, "See, I have nothing to hide."

Closed Hands

When someone is being deceitful or guarded, he tends to use hand and arm gestures less than usual. If he's sitting, he may keep his hands on his lap. If he's standing, he may keep them by his side, stuff them in his pockets, clutch an object tightly, or clench his fists. His gestures all seem to be saying,

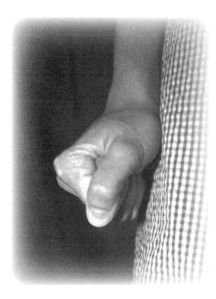

**A guarded or
hostile gesture**

"I'm holding on to something, and I'm not going to open up to you."

In negotiations a person about to make a sincere disclosure usually has both hands on the table and gestures as she speaks. Someone who is *not* going to be so forthright usually keeps her hands hidden under the table or close to her body. And watch for the person who, when asked a question, clenches her hands or turns her palms down. Chances are it's a sign of defensiveness and withdrawal.

I once asked a colleague how he was getting along with his new boss. "Oh, she's great," he replied, as he placed his hands in his pockets and immediately changed the subject. I found out several days later that he and his boss were having problems and that he was actively looking for another job.

Keeping their hands in their pockets is also a favorite ploy of men who don't want to participate in a conversation. Because hands do a lot of the communicating, putting them away sends the signal "I'm not going to say a word."

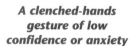

*A clenched-hands
gesture of low
confidence or anxiety*

Hand Gestures of Low Confidence

Signs that reflect levels of low confidence include hand
wringing and interlacing one's fingers. People who stick their
thumbs in their pockets or otherwise hide their thumbs are
usually demonstrating low confidence. (Most people leave
their thumbs in a neutral position, so any movement, up
or disappearing, could be significant.) Picking at the fingers of one hand with the other also shows discomfort or
low confidence.

Hand Gestures of High Confidence

It is common to see a person using one or more "steeple"
gestures (hands together, fingers interlocked, index fingers
raised and touching at the tips; or palms separated slightly,

*He's confident about
what he's saying.*

The look of comfort and confidence

fingers of both hands spread, and fingertips touching) when feeling confident or speaking comfortably about a subject he knows well. Politicians, executives, professors, and attorneys are very fond of using these gestures when they speak.

Sometimes businessmen hook their thumbs in the vest of their suit or hold the lapels of their suit to display confidence.

Hands of Resistance

Common hand gestures that express resistance or disagreement include nose, eye, and ear rubbing—body language for "That doesn't *smell* right to me," "That doesn't *look* right to me," or "That doesn't *sound* right to me." Tapping fingers on a table or desk is a sign of impatience. Leaning the chin on a hand with the index finger pointed up on the cheek usually indicates that the person is critical of the speaker or his subject. And the gesture of picking imaginary lint off clothes, whether conscious or not, conveys the message "I disagree with you, but I'm not going to argue about it."

A nonverbal sign of resistance

Some Other Hand Gestures

There are a number of other hand gestures that signal a variety of reactions.

Gestures of boredom   When the listener begins to use her hand (or hands) to support her head, she's telling you she's bored—and the more the hand supports the head, the greater the boredom.

She's lost interest.

Gestures of anger Gripping the hands behind the back often indicates anger or frustration.

Finger pointing Finger pointing and finger wagging are parental gestures of scolding, and I've often seen politicians and executives use this gesture in meetings, negotiations, or interviews for emphasis or to show dominance. The problem is that rather than being a sign of authority, aggressive finger pointing (with one or four fingers) suggests that the person is losing control of the situation, and it smacks of playground bullying.

A favorite gesture of the office bully

Gestures of interest Of course, not all gestures are negative. Genuine interest is shown when the hand lightly rests on the cheek and is not used for head support.

Chin stroking is a signal that the listener is evaluating what's been said. You need to look for the gesture that immediately *follows* the chin stroke. If the person leans forward, "steeples" his hands, or gives any other positive signal, the decision has most likely gone in your favor. If, however, he leans back and crosses his arms, you may be in trouble.

He's evaluating what you said, but his raised eyebrow says he's still skeptical.

Leaning in while placing hands palms down and patting them a few times on the table or desk (especially if accompanied by raised eyebrows) is almost always an indication of satisfaction.

Shoulder Positions

The position of the shoulders sends its own messages. There's a good reason, for example, that the phrase "He gave me the cold shoulder" is a metaphor for feeling rejected by someone. Shoulder muscles are vulnerable to even the slightest emotional shift, and a subtle change in posture (a dip, a hunch, or a forward or backward thrust) can give clues to a person's inner state. Watch and see if people's shoulders align with what they're verbalizing. Regardless of the words they may be using, here is what people's shoulders are telling you:

- People at ease have relaxed arms and shoulders— their shoulders drop forward slightly and their arms hang loose.

- Shoulders that are lifted and pulled back show control and alertness.

- Hunched shoulders may be simply bad posture or a sign of resignation and defeat.

- People signal that they are friendly and approachable when they relax one shoulder and cause it to drop below the other. This position can be taken by placing one hand in a pocket.

- Sometimes, however, uneven shoulders (where the level is noticeably different) indicate uncertainty. This is especially true when you see the shoulders alternating levels back and forth. It's a good guess that a person with this physical response is struggling to understand what was just said or is weighing her options before speaking.

Arms as Barriers

When someone is a stranger to the group or somewhat insecure, he or she often stands with partially crossed arms. In this subtler version of the crossed-arms gesture, one arm swings across the body to hold or touch the other arm. This forms a security barrier. A similar gesture, and one you'll see used by people standing before a crowd to accept an award or to give a speech, is hands clasped together in front of the body.

Another security barrier (this one favored by politicians, television personalities, salespeople, and others who don't want to appear nervous or unsure) is formed when one arm swings in front of the body so that the opposite hand can touch a shirt cuff, bracelet, watch, or other object on the arm. In fact, anytime you see someone move his arms across his body, chances are he's silently reassuring himself.

The Ultimate Closed Gesture

As a professional speaker, I hate to see the ultimate closed gesture in my audiences. It's the universal arms-crossed-over-the-chest position, and it carries the same defensive or negative meanings (disagreement, resistance, and guardedness) almost

The ultimate closed gesture

everywhere. But the crossed-arms gesture is more than just a not-so-encouraging audience posture. Research shows that when a listener folds his arms, not only does he have negative thoughts about the presenter but he's also paying less attention to what's being said.

In one study groups of volunteers were invited to attend a series of lectures. While doing so the first group was instructed to keep legs and arms uncrossed and to take a casual, relaxed sitting position. Volunteers in the second group were asked to attend the same lectures but to keep their arms tightly folded across their chests. The result showed that the folded-arms group learned and retained 38 percent less than the uncrossed-arms group.

TRY THIS

So, what should you do if you find yourself addressing an audience with crossed arms? Do *something* that encourages people to change position. I frequently open speeches by asking a series of questions to which audience members reply by raising their hands. In smaller meetings, I might have attendees break into couples or threesomes for a short discussion over a key issue. In a one-on-one encounter, I'd offer the individual a cup of coffee or tea (*you* try drinking with crossed arms!). There are other things you can do: hand out pens, books, brochures, samples, or a written quiz. It doesn't matter which strategy you choose so long as people have to uncross their arms to respond.

Note that it isn't only audience members who can embody this negative attitude. Last year I was on a panel of speakers and watched the man before me (representing a Fortune 100 company) finish his presentation and ask for questions—standing with his arms folded across his chest. Not surprisingly, the audience had no questions for him.

The Five C's of Gestures

In chapter 1 I listed the five C's necessary to decode body language. You need to understand how *context* changes meaning, look for gestural *clusters* that are sending the same message, notice if the nonverbal communication is *congruent* with the verbal message that accompanies it, know someone's baseline behavior so you can gauge *consistency*, and filter body language for *cultural* influences. Here are some examples of how these concepts apply to arm and hand gestures.

Context Consider a situation in which the audience members are sitting with their arms crossed in two meeting rooms. You might think that both meetings are filled with resisters, but when you compare their (physical) context you see a big difference. The temperature in the first room is chilly, and the chairs are armless. You know that both these circumstances encourage people to cross their arms for comfort. In the second room, the temperature is warm and the chairs have padded armrests. Now you have more cause to suspect that *here* there is resistance to what's being discussed.

Clusters A customer is trying to explain her frustration with a recent bank statement to you, the bank teller. She holds both hands open at chest level, palms up. Her shoulders are raised slightly, and her face has an expression of bewilderment. Looking closely, you see that the woman's body language is a cluster of signals of helplessness—and a genuine plea for assistance.

Congruence Your manager is giving some good advice about dealing with representatives of another company. "I want to finesse them on this deal," he says. But as he speaks, he pounds his fist on the desk. As a member of his staff, you hear what the manager says, but you also see his incongruent and aggressive gesture. You leave the meeting confused and unconvinced about what the manager really wants.

Consistency A woman is testifying at the fraud trial of her boss. Shaking from the time she takes the stand until she leaves the courthouse, the woman shows every classic non-verbal sign of dishonesty: no eye contact, hands touching her mouth and face and fiddling with her hair, and so on. But, as a courtroom observer, you know that this doesn't nec-essarily mean she is lying. (If she were, she would have prob-ably displayed more-comfortable body language in *some* part of her testimony—like when the attorney asked her routine questions about her professional background.) The fact that this woman's discomfort is consistent throughout her time in court shows that she's certainly agitated—but not neces-sarily dishonest.

Culture The American executive is jubilant at the end of a successful negotiation and flashes the thumbs-up gesture. Unfortunately, some of the attendees at the meeting are Aus-tralian. As one of them, you find that gesture highly offen-sive but you realize that in the executive's culture it is meant to signify "good job!"

That's a Wrap

Wrapping up a chapter on hand and arm gestures brings to mind the way directors wrap up a TV show—with the hand moving horizontally across the neck, for example, to signal "cut," or perhaps the gesture of the thumb and forefingers pulling away from each other as a sign to "stretch." They're familiar signals that send quick, well-understood messages.

Not so well understood are many of the hand signals I've described in this chapter, and that is why I encourage you to pay attention to them. You'll find that what people do with their hands tells you a lot more than they *realize* they're telling you. Then do everything you can to make what they have "said" work for you.

Feet First

FOR MILLIONS OF YEARS, our feet and legs have been our primary means of locomotion and in the forefront of responses to "fight, flight, or freeze" survival strategies. Our *limbic brain* (also called the *mammalian brain*) is at the center of our emotional response system. Its major function is to react instantaneously to incoming information from the environment. Emotional reactions, as we know, occur prior to thought. Before we've had time to develop any conscious plan, our limbic brain has already made sure that our feet and legs, depending on the situation, are geared to run away, kick out in defense, or freeze in place.

And we're hardwired for these reactions to threats. Although the hazards are very different in a modern business setting, whenever we are faced with something we perceive to be dangerous or even disagreeable, our feet and legs still respond in the same way: they freeze first, attempt to distance second, and finally, if no other alternative is available, prepare to fight and kick.

Joe Navarro worked for the FBI in behavioral analysis for fifteen years. Now he teaches body language skills to professional poker players. His advice? "I tell people to watch the feet, the hands, and the face—in that order. These are the most honest parts of the body."

Don't let the short length of this chapter fool you. It contains some of the most fascinating and useful clues for reading people. You'll discover how to spot anxiety, anticipation, welcome, exclusion, interest, and the desire to retreat—just by reading the signals sent by someone's legs and feet.

When people try to control their body language, they focus primarily on facial expressions and hand and arm gestures. Take politicians for example.

The major political parties train their candidates to project a favorable image of themselves and the party. Nonverbal communication plays a very significant role in establishing and maintaining this image. Politicians are coached to smile, make good eye contact, and cultivate a firm, warm handshake. When seated they are urged to adopt a forward-leaning posture that indicates a desire to cooperate with the listener in discussion.

But rarely is any public figure—politician, entertainer, or executive—coached in body language below the waist. And because gestures from the legs and the feet are left unrehearsed, they are also where the truth can most often be found. When it comes to reading nonverbal cues, professionals know that the feet, not the face, offer the most accurate and candid reflection of emotion.

Feet That Can't Stand to Lie

When lying, most people increase the number of times their feet move. Feet fidget, shuffle, and wind around each other or around the furniture. They stretch and curl to relieve tension. They may even wriggle or kick out in a symbolic attempt to run away.

You may not know it, but instinctively you've been reacting to foot gestures all your life. Studies show that observers, regardless of whether they realize they're "reading feet," have greater success exposing a person's falsehoods when they can see the entire body. No wonder so many business professionals are more comfortable interacting with others when a big desk hides their lower body!

TRY THIS

The next time you have a meeting with someone you want to evaluate or get to know better, get him out from behind the desk or conference table. Sit where you can view his entire body. Even if you don't do so consciously, you will pick up nonverbal cues from his feet and leg movements—cues that will add substantially to your overall understanding of the person.

Happy Feet

Our feet and legs not only react to stressors and threats but respond to positive emotions as well. "Dancing for joy," "kicking up your heels," "walking on air," and "staying on your toes" are some of the phrases used to acknowledge that positive connection.

Someone who plays cards regularly may know when one of his buddies has a good hand because, despite having assumed a noncommittal "poker face," the friend's twitching legs or bouncing feet always give him away.

Bouncing, tapping, wiggling feet are what professional poker players refer to as "happy feet." In poker it's a *high-confidence tell*—a signal that the player's hand is strong and opponents should beware.

There is a similar signal in business negotiations. If you see a lot of high-energy foot jiggling, or if you notice a slight bounce in the shoulders as a result of the movement, you can almost always assume that the party involved is feeling pretty good about his bargaining position.

In the opposite case, with a negotiator who is constantly bouncing her legs and suddenly stops right after she has presented an offer, it's probably a gesture of heightened anticipation—the equivalent of holding her breath.

Like any other nonverbal signal, bouncy feet need to be compared with a person's baseline. If someone has naturally jittery legs or feet (his normal reaction to stress), the happy feet signal is harder to detect.

Feet That Want to Be Somewhere Else

Imagine that you are sitting at the kitchen table with a three-year-old boy who would rather be outside playing. There he is, with his feet stretching to reach the floor even before he's finished eating. His upper body may be dutifully facing the table, but his legs and feet are already twisting and inching toward the door.

Think we give up this behavior as adults? Think again. It's ingrained. We may be more restrained but only marginally so. Our feet turn away from things we want to avoid, and they point in the direction we'd prefer to be going.

TRY THIS

Whenever you are speaking with a co-worker or client who seems to be paying attention, whose upper body is angled toward you but whose legs and feet have turned toward the door—look closer. If he jiggles or taps a foot, especially toward the exit, he may be symbolically running away.

Foot positions are revealing even if someone's legs are crossed. If the toe of the leg that is crossed is pointing toward you, the person is most likely with you emotionally. If the toe is pointing away, especially if it's pointing at the door, she is probably withdrawing.

Feet That Include or Exclude

Here's a common workplace situation you could find your-self facing: Two of your work colleagues are talking in the hallway. You'd like to join the conversation, but you don't know if you'll be seen as a rude interruption or a welcome addition.

You can find out—just by watching their feet.

When you approach the twosome, you will be acknowl-edged in one of two ways. If the feet of your two colleagues stay in place, and they twist only their upper torsos in your direction, they don't really want you to join the conversa-tion. But if their feet open to include you, you know that you are truly invited to participate. The feet nearest you will turn slightly in your direction—a position called *triangulation.*

Feet that exclude   **Feet that include**

TRY THIS

When you see a small group of people talking, look at their feet to see who's really connecting with whom. If all the feet triangulate or point to the common center of the group, it is an integrated conversation. If not, you'll be able to tell by the feet positions who is really in and who is being excluded.

Foot Lock

I was gathering background information for a change-management speech by interviewing various leaders at my client's company. Knowing that the impending change would have vast implications for her department, I was especially interested to talk with the head of customer service.

When I asked her, "How do you feel about the changes going on here?" the manager replied, "I have no problem. It's all fine with me." At which point she crossed her feet tightly at the ankles. "Are you sure?" I asked. She paused for a moment, uncrossed her ankles, and said, "Well, actually, I'm worried sick that we'll offshore this entire function."

A *foot lock* or *ankle lock,* in which a foot wraps around the opposite leg at the ankle or lower calf, is like having a "closed" sign hanging over the door.

As a therapist, I noticed that individuals who were not revealing information often locked their ankles and, when they finally allowed emotions to flow, they'd unlock their ankles. I've seen passengers who are nervous or uncomfortable during airplane takeoffs display the same foot-lock gesture. Human resource professionals notice that most interviewees

These feet show who feels included and who feels left out.

lock their feet at some point during the interview, indicating that they are holding back an emotion or attitude. And savvy negotiators look for foot locks as a possible sign that someone is holding back a valuable concession.

Foot locks also occur when people are feeling anxious or threatened. Most people lock their feet at the ankles when they sit in the dental chair. Another foot signal of insecurity or inferiority that you might see around the conference table is toes pointed inward. People may be sitting with the rest of the body open, but their feet are telling the real story.

Open and Closed Leg Positions

In general, open or uncrossed leg positions show an open or dominant attitude, whereas crossed positions are a sign of a closed attitude or uncertainly. People who are relaxed tend to take up more space with their legs. Sitting with legs apart in public is an especially masculine signal indicating a high level of comfort and confidence—although both men and women sit like this when they feel safe or unobserved. At a restaurant, with legs hidden by a tablecloth, both genders prefer this leg position.

Positions of comfort and confidence

Legs Crossed

There are many reasons for people to sit with their legs crossed. Often it is the most comfortable position to assume. Crossing legs at the knee with toes relaxed is the usual option for women. Both genders stretch out their legs and cross them loosely at the ankles, but men do this more often than women. Both poses are silent signals of casualness and ease.

Crossing one leg and resting it on the other thigh (so that the knee opens up) is a very masculine position that takes up a great deal of room and signals that the person is very sure of himself and of his place in the group.

The leg-lock position (a tightly closed leg cross that often accompanies the crossed-arms gesture) is the sitting posture used by many businesspeople who have a competitive nature. It is also a defensive signal used by most people when they are listening to something or someone they disagree with or feel threatened by.

On Bended Knee

"My knees went weak" is more than just an expression. It is a literal truth. In moments of extreme grief or despair, a person's knees may collapse and fail to hold their legs upright. So, when a police officer on *Law and Order* has to inform the victim's wife that her husband has been murdered, the first thing the officer says is "You'd better sit down." Collapsing knees are the body's way of saying, "I just can't stand it anymore."

Walk This Way

An individual's stride and pace indicate a variety of meanings, from confidence to depression. When a person is feeling down in the dumps, the head is bowed, the shoulders are stooped, and the person rarely looks up. Instead, the eyes gaze down and the walk is often lethargic. People who are feeling positive and confident usually have an evenly paced gait and look "light on their feet." Their posture is upright, their heads are straight, and their arms swing at their sides in an easy and relaxed manner.

Former U.S. president Ronald Reagan was called "the great communicator," and that included his use of body language. One newspaper reporter wrote that Reagan would emerge from behind a closed door in the White House, stride purposefully down a long red-carpeted corridor, then fairly bound onto a platform. His nonverbal message was one of vigor, authority, and ease.

I've seen executives walk into a conference room and project that same attitude. Those who do are telling everyone in the room, "I'm in charge here." And it's not by anything they say; the message is delivered by their confident walk, physical energy, and relaxed style.

People's training and background also affect how

A man "on the go"

they move. A professional dancer and a military officer carry themselves quite differently—even if both are female. But as unique as someone's profession and culture may make them, there are still some general signals you can pick up from watching people walk. Fast walkers look competent and busy. Speed and a lengthening stride correlate to a sense of urgency, and a "bounce in the step" signals an upbeat mood. You can even spot gender differences. Men tend to land squarely on their heels and roll toward the balls of their feet, and women catch their weight forward of their heels. Some women actually walk on the balls of their feet.

Standing Positions

There are six main standing positions, and each one tells you something about the attitude of the person assuming that position.

Standing at attention Junior officers addressing senior officers or employees talking to the boss most often assume this respectful, legs-together stance.

Standing with legs apart Like the seated legs-apart position, standing with legs apart and feet firmly planted on the ground is a predominantly male gesture (the western gunslinger pose) that signals dominance or determination. Putting hands on the hips or folding the arms while in this stance is a masculine gesture of power that also communicates coldness and inapproachability.

Standing with weight evenly distributed When people are comfortable, they usually balance their weight on both feet. The language that instinctively reflects this posture/attitude connection is "well balanced," "take a firm stand," and "knowing where you stand on this."

 **Standing with weight constantly shifting** When uncomfortable, many people fidget and shift their weight from one foot to the other. They may also rock back and forth as a way to calm themselves during anxious moments.

 **Standing with legs crossed** The crossed-legs stance is most often seen coupled with crossed arms. It's another closed and defensive posture that can also be a sign of low confidence. Many people stand in this position when they are in a group of strangers.

 **Standing with one foot forward** When the body weight is shifted to one hip, it leaves the lead leg and foot free to point in the direction of interest.

TRY THIS

At your next business function or social event, watch the different stances that people take. Can you pick out those who are uncomfortable or new to the group by the way they stand? (Most likely they stand with legs crossed or they shift their weight from foot to foot.)

When people are in a group, notice where the most feet are pointing. From that observation you can pick out the person who is the most important or interesting in the group—without hearing a word being spoken.

There's one more signal, it seems, that our feet send. I didn't see the need to include it earlier in this chapter, but I'll do it now—more as a public service and as one more reminder of how much we can learn from paying attention to feet.

It's most likely due to blood circulation, but it's apparently a well-known medical principle that warm feet are a sign of life. Not in *every* case, however, as evidenced by the 1899 death-bed story of John Holmes, the brother of Oliver Wendell Holmes. It seems that John fell into a coma and lay motionless for so long that his caretakers wondered whether he was still alive. One nurse, finding no pulse one day, felt his feet to see if they were warm.

"If they are, that means he's alive," she explained to the others in the room. "Nobody ever died with warm feet." The small group was stunned when the motionless John Holmes, his sense of humor intact till the very end, uttered his last words: "John Rogers did!"

John Rogers, you understand, was the first Protestant martyr in Mary Tudor's Roman Catholic reign. His feet, of course, were *very* warm when he died in 1555. He was burned at the stake.

CHAPTER 7

You're in My Space

HAVE YOU EVER FELT ANNOYED when you re-entered a meeting and found "your" seat taken by someone else? Have you felt offended when a co-worker entered your office without knocking or when you discovered your boss shuffling through papers on your desk?

Sure you have!

We all try to protect and control our space. It's called *territorial behavior,* and it is hardwired in our brains. In fact, territoriality is established so rapidly that even the second session in a series of lectures is sufficient to find most of the audience returning to their same seats.

In this chapter you'll see how the use of space in the workplace sends its own set of messages. You'll understand the impact of *spatial zones*—those distances between people that are most appropriate for various interactions—and why some people choose to disregard them. You'll see why seating arrangements are so important in business meetings and what someone's office can tell you about the person occupying it.

"I feel close to her."

"He is very standoffish."

"Back off!"

"She keeps me at arm's length."

Like facial expressions, hand gestures, and body postures, space *speaks*. And *proxemics*—the study of space as used in nonverbal communication—says volumes about relationships. People communicate through the distances they maintain during encounters.

TRY THIS

At your next business meeting, notice who sits next to whom. Most of the time, people choose to sit near others they like and agree with about the topic to be discussed. They will also find ways to put distance between themselves and those they dislike.

Spatial Zones

A salesman was taking a client out to lunch, and by the time they'd finished their drinks at the bar, I knew the deal was lost. I watched the salesman move so close to his prospect that the client began, very slowly, to inch away. When the client could stand it no longer, he excused himself to make a phone call—and left the restaurant shortly thereafter.

One of the easiest mistakes to make during an encounter with someone is to misjudge how much space the other person needs to feel comfortable. A mistake here can trigger a truly deep-seated response. Anthropologist Edward T. Hall was one of the pioneers in the study of proxemics (in fact, he coined the word), and he found that people's territorial responses are deeply rooted and primitive. They are also predictable—if you know what to look for.

There are five zones in which people feel most comfortable in dealing with one another. One way to think of these is as a set of invisible bubbles we all carry with us into the workplace.

Intimate zone (0 to 18 inches)   This zone is reserved for family and loved ones. Within this zone we embrace, touch, and whisper. This close contact is appropriate only for very personal relationships.

Close personal zone (1½ to 2 feet)   This is the bubble most people in the United States like to keep around us. This zone is used for interactions among friends or familiar and trusted business partners.

Far personal zone (2 to 4 feet)   This zone is for interactions we prefer to conduct at arm's length. In this zone we can communicate interest without the commitment of touching.

Social zone (4 to 12 feet)   The social zone is most appropriate for the majority of daily business interactions. It is where we interact with new business acquaintances or at more formal social affairs.

Public zone (more than 12 feet)   This zone is mostly used for public speaking.

All these zones are, of course, invisible to us and to others, but that doesn't make them any less real. Few of us are comfortable in a crowded subway train or elevator, where we are forced into an intimate distance with people we don't know. In those cases, we usually look straight ahead and avoid making eye contact. And as strangers edge into our personal space, we will often lean or move away from them in an attempt to create an acceptable distance.

The amount of space required to feel comfortable varies from individual to individual. People who don't like being touched tend to keep their distance from others. People who touch others while talking want to get close enough to do so.

And, of course, space can also vary depending on the amount of trust in a relationship. The greater the distance, the lower the level of trust.

We also make assumptions about relationships based on zones. If we see two people talking at a distance of about two feet from each other, we assume they are engaged in the kind of conversation possible only between those who know each other well. So, their spatial relationship becomes part of what is being communicated.

Gender also plays an important role. Men who don't know each other well tend to keep a greater distance between them than women who have just met. This difference in interpersonal distance as determined by gender is even true in Web 2.0's virtual online worlds (such as Second Life and social networking sites), where many of the rules that govern personal space in the physical world can be found in the virtual world.

TRY THIS

Whether you work in an office building, a factory, or a department store, you have many opportunities to observe people in workplace conversations. As you do, notice the distance that separates them. See if you can guess the trust level between co-workers by the spatial zones they occupy when interacting.

It's also interesting to note that we all allow some people to get closer to us than others. Research from the University of Arizona finds that those who have positive qualities (attractive, well dressed, higher status) are more easily able to invade other people's space. And, of course, some professionals—beauticians, personal trainers, doctors, and massage therapists—routinely encroach on our personal space. As a dental hygienist noted, "The practice of dentistry throws the notion of proxemics out the window. The idea of one's 'intimate zone' is completely ignored and abused, as we all know when someone is poking and scraping in our mouths. In those special circumstances, there is an unstated agreement between patient and dental practitioner that the laws of proxemics will be suspended. But as soon as treatment is completed and the patient is upright again, the rules resume immediately."

Business Zone

Most U.S. business relationships begin in the social zone. As the relationships develop and trust is formed, both parties may subconsciously decrease the distance to the personal zone. But if one of the parties moves too close too soon, it can result in a communication breakdown.

When people are not aware of these zones and the meanings attached to them, unintentional violations may occur, resulting in discomfort and distrust. Those who feel powerful often display their confidence by taking up a large amount of physical space. In so doing they may unknowingly infringe on another person's territory.

Of course, violating someone's personal space can also be deliberate—to *create* discomfort. Police interrogators often use the strategy of sitting closely and crowding a suspect. This theory of interrogation assumes that invasion of the suspect's

Too close for comfort

personal space, with no chance for defense, will give the officer a psychological advantage.

In the one-upmanship that is all too often part of organizational life, I've watched high-ranking executives purposefully stand too close, to make a competitor feel self-conscious
or uncomfortable. I've seen managers crowd staff members
to emphasize their status in the organization.

But regardless of their motive, anyone who comes too
close to you in an undesirable way triggers a physiological
reaction: your heart rate and galvanic skin responses increase.
You then try to restore the proper distance by withdrawing
and retreating. You may look away, pull back to create space,
step behind a barrier (desk, chair, or table), tuck in your chin
toward your chest in an instinctive move of protection, or
even rub your neck so that your elbow protrudes sharply
toward the invader. This shows that proximity is a powerful
nonverbal force and that most people need to increase their
sensitivity in using it.

Again, regardless of motive, people who overstep our
space boundaries are perceived as either overly aggressive or
socially clueless. Getting too close is an especially improper
business move in circumstances where co-workers, colleagues,
or clients are in danger of feeling emotionally or physically
threatened by the invasion of their personal space.

TRY THIS

Notice how you react when someone gets too close to you—and try to guess his motive for invading your space. (Is he attempting to intimidate you? To impress you with his status? Or is he simply unaware?)

Space and Status

Space in the workplace often indicates dominance and leadership. The higher the professional status an employee has, the more space he or she is commonly awarded. Another difference can be seen in how close one approaches the desk or chair of another. People who enter a room but remain near the door signal lower status than those who walk all the way in. In fact, whether we know it or not, we generally judge people to have low confidence or little power when they keep an increased distance from us, while we associate high confidence and more power with a willingness to get physically closer.

As mentioned, another way that status is demonstrated nonverbally in a meeting is by physically taking up space (claiming your territory). Lower-status, less-confident men (and most women) tend to pull in. They keep all their materials in one neat pile, whereas more-confident or higher-status men will usually spread out their papers and claim their turf.

In meetings the person with high status is usually seated at the end of a table (the power position). When a new

"We're reorganizing our infrastructure. Everyone move two chairs to the left."

person enters the room, he will often adjust his jacket, touch his hair, or make other adjustments to how he looks. This lets the person in power know subconsciously that the person entering cares about how he presents himself. Senior staff members often sit to the right of their boss at the head of the table—perhaps the origin of the term *right-hand man.*

TRY THIS

In any meeting you might be hosting, keep the desired goal in mind and choose the setting carefully. A boardroom will probably have a large rectangular or oval table, creating space for higher-status people to sit at the head, and thereby control the agenda, and giving the meeting a formal and businesslike feeling. But for a meeting in which you want collaboration and participation, you probably wouldn't want such a pronounced hierarchical arrangement, nor would you want the rest of the team sitting across from one another in adversarial positions. The rule of thumb here is: if you want to foster a competitive element, place opponents on opposite sides of the table; if you want to stimulate collaboration, seat people side by side.

*"Ladies! Gentlemen! Arm wrestling
never solved anything!"*

Take a Seat

People's seating arrangements can shape their interactions by allowing or blocking eye contact and visibility of other non-verbal cues. Seating positions may even help create leaders. For example, people who sit at either end of the table in a jury room are more likely to be elected foreperson.

One experiment randomly assigned college males to sit in particular seats at a table. The researchers arranged it so that more people were seated at one half of the table, and only two people sat on the opposite side—and these two seats were considered "visually central" because their occupants would be highly observed from the more crowded side. As was predicted, occupants of the visually central seats received the highest ratings in leadership after discussions had taken place.

Of course, this study raises more questions than it answers: Were the two men really leaders, or was it the seating arrangement that allowed others to perceive them that way? Or did the two men begin to act differently because they felt they had the central position and it was their job to speak up? It's hard to know exactly what happened, but it might be interesting to experiment with seating at your next meeting and draw you own conclusions.

TRY THIS

If you are having dinner with a business partner, find a table that allows you to sit at right angles to each other. It may have a positive impact on the quality of your conversation. Research shows that people are more interactive when seated at right angles than when straight across from each other.

I often speak in front of audiences in theater-style, straight-row seating. But when the meeting planner gives me a choice (and when the audience is small enough—say, less than three hundred—to accommodate it), I always request round tables of six to eight people. Here's why: I like a lot of audience interaction. In straight-row seating, the location of participants is a major factor in determining how individuals respond and how involved they are. (Research shows that, in such an arrangement, participant interaction is greatest in the front and middle rows, regardless of whether the seating is imposed or self-selected.) With tables, I can encourage small-group discussions and then take a wireless microphone into the audience and get reactions from anywhere in the room.

TRY THIS

If your objective for a meeting is to stimulate teamwork, find a round table, where everyone can sit in a circle. This arrangement sends a nonverbal signal of equality and facilitates communication among participants. The legendary King Arthur understood the power of this arrangement when he chose a round table for his knights. That way no one had higher status than anyone else.

Objects as Barriers

Another way that people use space to send nonverbal messages is to fill it with things they can hide behind. People often use objects as barriers when they are uncomfortable with what is being said, when they feel they are being coerced, or when they otherwise feel the need for protection.

Norma, a manager I was coaching, used to hide from my critique by creating a physical barrier between the two of us. She was quite relaxed and open so long as my comments about her leadership skills were positive, but whenever I discussed an area that needed improvement, Norma would unconsciously begin to line up objects (coffee cup, books— even her purse!) on the desk in front of her.

Office Layout

I've often noticed that executives communicate their attitudes about power and status by the way they utilize their office space. If you walk into someone's office and find a conversation area (chairs of equal size set around a small table or at right angles to each other), you'll probably infer that the occupant likes to speak with guests more casually and personally than he or she could from behind a desk. That office layout tells you that the person is informal and most likely collaborative. On the other hand, the message you get from someone who conducts all interactions from behind a large desk, with his or her guests seated in smaller (and almost always more uncomfortable) chairs stationed in front of the desk, is one of control or superiority.

Of course, not everyone is an executive and not all offices or workspaces have enough room for a separate conversation area. But many offices could be made more inviting to guests by simply moving the visitor's chair to the side rather than in front of the desk.

Savvy leaders know the power of office layout as a metaphor for workplace relationships. That's why many successful businesspeople choose not to speak with clients, customers, or employees from behind a desk but instead come around the desk and sit next to them. A manager in a manufacturing company uses this strategy with new employees: "When I first meet with members of my staff, I pull my chair to the opposite side of the desk so that we are sitting next to one another. I tell them that sometimes I may physically be seated behind my desk, but that this is the way I think of us—as partners working side by side."

This arrangement divides people.

This arrangement brings people together.

Contrast that with the senior project manager who conducted meetings in his office by placing a worktable perpendicular to the front of his desk. He sat in a comfortable chair behind his desk while the rest of the "team" sat in armless chairs at the table. This arrangement allowed the manager to reinforce his role as the authority figure in the room. In the words of one participant in those meetings, "There he'd be, leaning back in his big chair, while the rest of us sat upright at the table. We felt like peasants who'd been summoned by the lord of the manor!"

TRY THIS

If you want to use your office space to enhance a conversation, don't put any object between you and the person with whom you're talking. Move out from behind your desk when you want a real dialogue and stay behind the desk only when maintaining control is more important than exchanging information.

Workplace Design

The layout of your organization sends its own nonverbal messages. Here's an example of one company that used design to encourage collaboration. At Caterpillar's European headquarters in Geneva, Switzerland, employees represent a mixture of nationalities from all over the world. While essential for a successful global operation, this diversity complicates communication: not only are employees dealing with multiple languages and backgrounds but they're interacting with people who come from very different cultures. The challenge was how to make this diverse population think of themselves as a team.

A few years ago, Caterpillar's employee communication manager, Gottardo Bontagnali, kept thinking about the role played by the central market square—*piazza* in Italian—in virtually all European villages. In addition to going there for necessities of daily life, villagers went to exchange news, pick up gossip, pass on information, and socialize. It was, and in many places still is, the village's most efficient communication tool.

So Bontagnali decided to create a "piazza" at Caterpillar's Geneva headquarters, based on the village theme. Local artists were brought in to paint the walls of the top-floor cafeteria with large village scenes—dotted with bright yellow Cat machines, of course—as well as sights from multiple Cat locations. And the villagers portrayed in the panoramas were actual Cat employees. The result was amazing: with a little imagination, you could actually picture yourself in a European market square surrounded by familiar sights and faces.

Employees were then encouraged to use the piazza for informal meetings and discussions. "Let's discuss it over a cup of coffee in the piazza" has now become part of Caterpillar's business culture in Geneva. And because so many people use it for regular exchanges, it's become an important means of sharing information on an impromptu basis as well. But the most impressive result is how workplace design helped build workforce camaraderie and a common sense of purpose.

In a completely different type of enterprise, AdFarm, a Canadian advertising agency, uses workplace design to symbolize organizational values. According to Art Froehlich, a senior partner with the firm: "In our organization the owners have windowless offices, and staff members are assigned the nicer rooms with views. No one has a corner office. All those are turned into meeting rooms. Using space this way is one way we communicate our values to employees. And, by the way, we've been chosen as one of the fifty best workplaces in Canada."

Using space, creating your own space, or invading someone else's space can, as we've seen, play a critical role in how we interact in business situations.

It's been decades since space exploration began and the first Russian and American satellites orbited the Earth. As it applies to professional relationships, however, it seems that we are on the frontier of a different "Space Age." Make *that* exploration work for you by understanding the messages that are being sent—and need to be respected—when people use space and distance as part of their workplace communication.

The Power of Touch

Usually considered the most primitive—and essential—form of nonverbal communication, touching begins with a baby's first cuddle. The power of touch is so basic and so effective that clinical studies at the Mayo Clinic show that premature babies who are stroked grow 40 percent faster than those who do not receive the same amount of touching. Touch is used worldwide as an integral part of childcare, courtship, and comfort.

In business, touch is the quickest way to establish personal rapport. This chapter explores touch, or *haptics,* as the study of touching is called, in professional settings. You'll learn why positive emotional reactions can be triggered by a single touch, how to use touch to create emphasis and hold attention, the nonverbal signals that say "don't touch," and how to create the most positive impression when you shake someone's hand.

If you found a coin, would you give it to a person who approached you and said it was hers? Would it make any difference if the person approaching you touched your arm when she made the request?

Well, no—and yes! Only 23 percent of the unsuspecting subjects set up in this experiment by researchers at the

University of Minnesota admitted that they had found the money when asked. But if the researcher touched the elbow of the subject when inquiring about the coin, the percentage of those admitting possession rose to 68 percent—and they often looked embarrassed, with explanations like, "I was just looking around to see who lost the money."

High Touch

We are programmed to feel closer to someone who's touched us. The person who touches also feels more connected. It's a powerful force, and even momentary touching can create a human bond. A touch on the forearm that lasts a mere one-fortieth of a second can make the receiver not only feel better but also see the giver as being kinder and warmer. The person who's been touched also perceives the environment as friendlier.

The right kind of touch at the right time can even make you money! Research by the Cornell University School of Hotel Administration concludes that being touched by servers increases the tips that customers leave. At two informal restaurants, waitresses were assigned customers who were randomly divided into three categories. Some customers were not touched at all, others were touched once on the shoulder for about one and a half seconds, and the rest were touched twice on the palm of the hand for about a half second each. All touches were given casually as the waitress returned change to the customer at the end of the meal. In all cases, eye contact was avoided.

The results at both restaurants were significant. Customers who weren't touched left an average tip of 12 percent. Tips increased to 14 percent from those who were touched on the shoulder and to 17 percent from those touched twice on the hand.

TRY THIS

If you're among the nearly 2 million people who work as wait staff in the United States, give touching a try. Remember to touch lightly and briefly on the shoulder or the palm of the hand. Then compare your results with these research findings:

▶ Casually touching customers increases the tips of both male and female servers.

▶ Touching increases tips more when waitresses touch the female members of mixed-sex couples than when they touch the men.

▶ Touching increases the tips from young customers more than those from older customers.

But it isn't only in restaurants that customers respond favorably to being touched. In many commercial settings, casually touching customers has been shown to increase the time they spend in a store, the amounts they purchase, and the favorable evaluation of their shopping experience. It was observed that supermarket customers who had been touched were more likely to taste and purchase food samples than were customers who were not touched. Touch has also been found to increase the number of people who volunteered to score papers and sign petitions.

ANDERSON

"Tell you what, rub my tummy and it's a deal."

To Touch or Not to Touch—
That Is the Question

Bill is the head of marketing for a telecommunications company—and a natural toucher. As such, he utilizes an interesting and effective (but not uncommon) communication technique. When he speaks he touches the listener (almost always on the forearm) to add emphasis to key parts of his statements. Touching ensures that, for a moment, he has someone's full attention. Because touch is used most often when we believe strongly in something (a liar rarely touches the person he is talking to), Bill's touching also subconsciously enhances his credibility.

But in Anglo-Saxon cultures, especially the United States and the United Kingdom, touching colleagues is far less common than in some other parts of the world. In our sensitivity to political correctness, we may have lost a potent way to connect with others. Sometimes the simple act of touching someone to show support, encouragement, agreement, sympathy, or gratitude adds the personal warmth to our communication that is otherwise lacking.

I was reminded of this when I was coaching Suzanne. Suzanne was the leader of an information technology department—a brilliant "techie," struggling to develop better interpersonal communication skills. After watching Suzanne in one-on-one conversations with various business managers—and seeing the dismissive way most of the managers treated her—I was wondering how to help her command their attention. And then I saw it: In one conversation Suzanne was so intent on what she was saying that she leaned forward and touched her colleague's arm. What a difference that single touch made! The manager looked up at Suzanne as though seeing her for the first time. And, more importantly, he began to really listen to what she was saying.

> **TRY THIS**
>
> Try increasing your communication impact by adding a touch now and again—but remember to use your common sense about proper behavior in a professional setting. Here are a few things to keep in mind:
>
> ▶ Look for signs of discomfort. People signal a reluctance to be touched by crossing their arms and legs, pulling back, and buttoning or holding on to their jackets.
>
> ▶ Limit the contact to the hands, arms, shoulders, and back. And be aware that touching bare shoulders or backs— which female summer attire may expose—can be perceived as a personal rather than a business gesture.
>
> ▶ Make the touch light and short (only long enough to establish a positive nonverbal signal) and then step back.

Who Touches Whom?

Political and symbolic messages are expressed and reinforced by various forms of touch—and their avoidance. Directly touching people with special status is often off-limits, and to breech this boundary is a sign of disrespect or defiance. There was an outcry a few years ago when the Australian prime minister lightly touched Queen Elizabeth II on her visit to Australia. While defended as a token of hospitality, many British citizens took it as a flagrant insult to royalty.

In most business environments and organizations, touching is a nonverbal signal of the boss/subordinate relationship. And in most cases, it's the boss who does the touching. It is quite common (and usually favorably accepted) for a manager to touch the shoulder, upper back, or arm of an employee while saying, "Good job!" It is far less common for the employee to act in kind.

Like any other nonverbal cue, touch can be misused as a manipulation or power play. Some people may use touch to display a sense of control or one-upmanship, and in those cases a touch can feel condescending and uncomfortable and be unwelcome.

Touch That Conveys Ownership

Touching behaviors in the workplace extend to office furniture, and sometimes this kind of touch is unwelcome. People touch or lean against objects to show possession or ownership. But when the object (a desk or file cabinet) belongs to someone else, touching or leaning against it can be taken as a gesture of intimidation.

Depending on the relationship, touching or sitting on another person's desk can be a signal of intimacy or intimidation.

TRY THIS

Start paying attention to the amount of touching that is acceptable in your organization's culture. Notice who the touchers are and the positive or negative responses they get. Be aware of people coming into your workspace or office who touch or lean on objects there—and notice your own reaction to their displays of familiarity. You may be amazed to discover how much touch plays a part in your daily work life!

Handshakes

Hand gestures as greetings originated in our early prehistory—perhaps to show that no weapons were carried. Today the North American handshake is the universally understood business greeting. The handshake is the most formal and least personal of the touch gestures, but it has great importance, especially in initial interactions and after long absences.

Physical touch and warmth are established through the handshaking tradition, and this tactile contact makes a lasting impression. It may well be what someone remembers most about meeting you. The thing to keep in mind is that the purpose of a handshake is to greet someone, say goodbye, express congratulations, or signal agreement on a deal. As such it should be perceived as warm, friendly, and sincere.

Handshakes can be described by the nature of the grip, the pressure of the grip, the number of times one pumps the other's hand, and even how far apart people stand when they shake hands.

It's just a touch, but every handshake sends a powerful message.

TRY THIS

Watch people in your organization as they shake hands during business exchanges. You'll notice that in a classic, ceremonial handshake, people usually stand about two feet apart and extend their arms. As a relationship develops, you'll see the handshake last longer and the distance between the participants close by several inches, causing their arms to bend more at the elbows.

People will often make personality judgments based on the kind of handshake used. I've seen a weak handshake mark someone as "too timid for a sales position." Conversely, the "bone crusher"—a macho handshake in which a person squeezes too tightly—can give the impression of being overbearing or insensitive. Neither of these stereotypes is without notable exceptions, of course. I've known several tough-as-nails business negotiators who had the lightest of grips. So be careful not to put too much emphasis on evaluating a person's character by the way he or she shakes your hand.

Valid indicators or not, people *do* constantly evaluate each other by the way they shake hands. Here are a few other common handshakes—and how they are most often interpreted.

The dead fish   A cold, clammy, and limp handshake sends the nonverbal message "I'm nervous, insecure, or timid."

The finger grinder   Similar to the bone crusher, and sending a similar aggressive message, this is the handshake where one party squeezes the fingers of the other.

The stiff arm   When someone offers a straight-arm handshake, creating more distance between himself and the other person, it's processed as distrust, aloofness, or reserve.

The glove   This is the typical politician's handshake, where two hands reach out to clasp and surround another's hand, like a glove. Because the glove handshake has been so widely associated with diplomatic, political, and business dealings—and because the credibility of these professions has plummeted—its interpretation has morphed from a gesture of sincere liking to one of faked concern.

Mr. President, Meet Mr. President

It's a matter of personal style, of course, but both George W. Bush and Bill Clinton have unique handshaking techniques. President Bush tends to keep his legs slightly apart and to lean in with his upper body when shaking hands. He habitually touches people on the shoulder or the elbow and lets his touch linger there. President Clinton shakes your hand with his right hand and with his left hand pulls you in by your elbow. Because of the increased element of intimacy, both presidents' greetings are perceived as warmer and more personal than a traditional politician's handclasp.

Let's Shake on It!

You extend your hand and reach for someone else's hand to shake. It's the simplest of nonverbal exchanges and one you may engage in several times a day. But hidden within such a seemingly simple formality is an opportunity to make a lasting impression. A study on handshakes by the Income Center for Trade Shows showed that people are two times more likely to remember you if you shake hands with them. The trade-show researchers also found that people react to those with whom they shake hands by being more open and friendly. Various other studies show that shaking hands makes you more likable, friendly, and persuasive.

Here are some rules to keep in mind so that you can convey a positive message at first touch:

- When shaking hands, look directly into the other person's eyes.

- Smile.

- Stand when being introduced to someone and when extending your hand.

- Make sure your right hand is free to shake hands. Always shift a briefcase, papers, beverage, or cell phone to your left hand before you begin the greeting so that your handshaking hand is ready for action.

- Keep your body squared off to the other person—facing him or her fully.

- Make sure you have palm-to-palm contact and that the web of your hand touches the web of the other person's. Research with salespeople indicates that if customers don't get this full-palm contact, they wonder what the other person is hiding. If so, they may remain uncomfortable for the rest of the interaction and be less likely to purchase.

- Offer your hand with your palm facing sideways. When a person offers his hand with the palm faced upward, it is considered a submissive gesture. Conversely, when someone offers his hand with the palm faced downward (or twists his hand downward during the handshake), it sends a message of superiority. But people who offer a sideways hand to shake send a message of equality and confidence.

- Shake hands firmly, especially if you are female. Women with a firm handshake make a more favorable impression and are judged to be confident and assertive.

- Hold the other person's hand a few fractions of a second longer than you are naturally inclined to do. This conveys additional sincerity and quite literally holds the other person's attention while you exchange greetings.

- Start talking before you let go: "It's great to meet you" or "I'm so glad to be here."

- Make sure that when you break away, you do not look down (it's a submissive signal).

In today's litigious, cover-your-behind, *i*-dotting and *t*-crossing society—especially a business environment where e-mails and blind copies contribute to a culture of blame and mistrust—there remains the world of New York diamond traders, where much of their business is done on a handshake. Something about that must make them feel pretty good.

CHAPTER 9

Translating Body Language across Cultures

When we talk about culture, we're generally talking about a set of shared values that a group of people hold. Such values affect how members of that group think and act and, more importantly, the kind of criteria by which they judge others. Cultural meanings render some behaviors as "normal" and "right" and others as "strange" or "wrong." From greeting behaviors to hand gestures to the use of space and touch, what's proper and correct in one culture may be ineffective—or even offensive—in another.

Few of us are aware of our own cultural biases because cultural imprinting begins at a very early age. And though some of a culture's values are taught explicitly, most are absorbed subconsciously. Often it is our lack of awareness and subconscious biases that create problems when we are trying to translate body language across cultures.

The goal of this chapter is not to describe all the body language variances around the world but rather to help you become aware of the cultural values behind those variances. You'll gain insight into some of the basic cultural divisions and the nonverbal signals you can generally expect to find within those divisions. You will learn how cultures differ in their comfort with touching and personal space, how "context" cultures approach business differently than "content" cultures, and why displaying feelings in the workplace is judged differently in affective and neutral cultures. You'll also learn why talking with your hands can get you into trouble and how greeting behaviors, eye contact, and head-nod cues can change meaning from culture to culture.

Differences and Commonalities

Basically, there are two kinds of body language signals: acquired and instinctive. *Acquired* gestures are socially generated, so identical gestures often have different meanings among different societies. For example, in most European countries the correct way to wave hello and good-bye is palm out, hand and arm stationary, fingers wagging up and down. Common North American waving, with the hand moving side to side means "no" throughout Mediterranean Europe and Latin America. In Peru that gesture means "come here." Called the *moutza* in Greece, that same gesture is a serious insult, and the closer the hand is to the other person's face, the more threatening it is considered to be.

But if acquired behaviors showcase our differences, our commonality is displayed in *instinctive* body language. The eyebrow flash is one example of an instinctive gesture that is shared by all human beings. People around the world automatically raise their eyebrows and wrinkle their foreheads when they greet one another. And then, of course, there are the six universal facial expressions (joy, sadness, surprise, fear, disgust/contempt, and anger).

As you get deeper into this chapter on cultural differences, remember that we human beings also have much in common! Also keep in mind that we are all individuals and that no two people belonging to the same culture will necessarily respond in exactly the same way. Generalizations are valid only to the extent that they provide clues on what you will *most likely* encounter when dealing with members of a particular culture.

TRY THIS

When preparing for an international business trip, it's a good idea to study the specific culture you'll be dealing with, but remember that books or articles on the global protocol may offer advice that is generalized or stereotypical. The best guideline still is: when in Rome, do as the Romans do. Or, as I paraphrase it: stay aware and copy what you see!

Global Business Protocol

I recently received a phone call from the meeting planner for a pharmaceutical company. She wanted me to participate in a panel discussion on global business protocol. "And," the meeting planner told me, "don't worry about giving us information you think might be too basic. We need all the help we can get!"

As globalization has become a fact of business life, cultural acumen is becoming a required skill. Today everyone is part of the global marketplace, and business professionals may be required to deal with their counterparts in other countries or lead a multicultural team. And, at least for most business professionals in the United States, we still have a lot to learn and a long way to go.

An example of the role of nonverbal communication in the broader area of global protocol is this American organization that was hoping to impress a group of businessmen from

**"We're not adapting quickly to the new global
economy. But yesterday I had Mexican food for lunch,
and today I'm having Chinese. It's a start!"**

Japan. It was an important evening for the civic leaders of a
midwestern city. The local chamber of commerce was hosting a dinner for the Japanese executives, who were considering locating a factory in that city. And everything seemed to
go wrong.

The cultural mishaps started when the chamber president was formally introduced to the top-ranking Japanese
executive. The president held out this hand for a shake; the
Japanese chairman bowed. The president then hastily bowed,
while his Japanese counterpart thrust out his hand. To the
embarrassment of all, this gestural dance continued for several minutes.

Then things got worse.

When everyone was finally seated for dinner, the welcoming gifts for members of the Japanese contingent
were opened. They were lovely pocketknives, handsomely
engraved with the name of the Japanese company. Unfortunately, the gift givers didn't realize that knives are a Japanese
symbol suggesting suicide.

By the end of the evening, the city officials had managed
to offend all their guests—without saying a word.

> ### TRY THIS
>
> You can begin to prepare for whatever country you're doing business with by creating a list of body language rules for doing business in your own culture. A list of such rules might include "look people in the eye," "shake hands firmly," and "don't crowd people." And, remember, you are not labeling these behaviors as right or wrong; you are simply stating your culture's norms. *Then* do some research to learn how these gestures are interpreted in the country you'll be visiting.

Contact versus Noncontact Cultures

Cultures can be categorized in many ways, but one of the most obvious variations (and one that can be potentially uncomfortable for business professionals) is the amount of touching that a culture feels is appropriate. Take my first business trip to South America as an example.

I was booked to speak at a change-management conference in Venezuela. Miguel, the meeting planner I knew through e-mail correspondence and telephone conversations, met me at the Caracas airport. He greeted me with a soft, lingering handshake and then a hug and a kiss on the cheek. As we walked toward the waiting car and driver, Miguel stayed by my side and put his hand on my shoulder. He sat close to me in the backseat of the car, and as we discussed the upcoming program, he often touched my arm or hand.

If this had been your experience, how would you have evaluated Miguel's nonverbal behavior?

The "right" answer, of course, varies depending on which cultural standards you use when judging and what those standards reflect about touching and being touched.

In general, *contact* cultures such as France, Latin America, Israel, Greece, and Saudi Arabia use a greater frequency of touch cues than do *noncontact* cultures such as Germany, the United Kingdom, Japan, and North America. In many cultures touching someone on the arm to make a point as you speak or putting a hand on their shoulder—or even on their hand—are gestures of trust or approval. In others this same behavior is considered excessive, overly familiar, or even sexual harassment.

The differences in touch frequency showed up in one study where conversations in outdoor cafés (in Miami, Florida; London, England; and San Juan, Puerto Rico) were observed and the number of times people gave or received casual touches was counted. A total of 189 touches per hour were recorded in San Juan and two per hour in Miami. In London during that same hour? None.

So, what might you expect when dealing with business professionals in contact cultures? Expect that some individuals may get up close and personal: Your Mexican associate may want to embrace you at the end of a long and successful business meeting. So might your central and eastern European associates, who are just as likely to give you a bear hug *and* kiss you three times on alternating cheeks. Indian businessmen might show their appreciation by enthusiastically slapping you on the back.

Also expect to encounter individuals whose behavior does not conform. Remember, not all people in a culture act in the same way. And even among contact cultures, there are differences in the rules governing touch behavior. For example, in Arab cultures two people of the same gender may greet each other with a kiss on each cheek or walk together linking arms or holding hands. Colleagues of different genders in a professional setting, however, will tend not to touch at all.

Cultures and Spatial Relationships

The comfort level of people from different cultures also differs measurably when it comes to physical space. Members of some cultures formally distance themselves from one another when doing business, getting close only to shake hands or exchange business cards. In the United States, for instance, most people engaged in conversation with a new business acquaintance will assume a social distance of roughly 4 to 7 feet. In many other parts of the world, however, the expected social distance is roughly half that—or even closer. Many cultures compress the space between people even more so that they are close enough to touch each other (lightly gripping another's arm, touching the lapel of another's jacket, or sometimes briefly hugging) during business dealings.

I once watched (with great amusement) as a Spanish businessman backed his English colleague all the way across a conference room. Here's how it looked: As the two talked, the Spaniard would move close to the Englishman until there were only a few inches separating the two. The Englishman would then step back to create a greater distance between them. This cross-cultural tango continued for several minutes—the Spaniard moving in and the Englishman stepping back. The amusing part to me was, because their conversation was so intent, neither man seemed to notice that they had traveled from one end of the room to the other.

As a rule, southern cultures value intimacy in business relationships, and northern cultures tend to prefer distance. So, in Latin cultures people tend to be more comfortable standing close to one another; in Nordic cultures the opposite is true. Americans often stand farther apart than their Latin and Arab associates but closer than their Asian counterparts. Recognizing these spatial preferences helps eliminate the discomfort people may feel if the interpersonal distance is too great (standoffish) or too close (intrusive and pushy). It might also help you avoid being backed across a conference room!

Context versus Content Cultures

In *context* cultures (Mediterranean, Slavic, central European, Latin American, African, Arab, Asian, and American Indian), much of the message is left unspecified—to be understood through the relationship of the participants, the nonverbal cues they send, and a between-the-lines interpretation of what is actually said. By contrast, in *content* cultures (most of the Germanic and English-speaking countries) messages are expected to be explicit and specific. The former are looking for meaning and understanding in what is *not* said—in body language, in silences and pauses, and in relationships and empathy. The latter place emphasis on sending and receiving accurate messages directly and by being precise with spoken or written words.

People from context cultures tend to view personal bonds and informal agreements as far more binding than any formal contract. People from content cultures don't believe the deal is finalized until everyone has signed on the dotted line. And therein lies the potential for conflict.

When Lee Iacocca was running Ford Motor Company, he wanted to buy Ferrari. Some of Iacocca's top people went to see Enzo Ferrari, and they came to an understanding: Ford would acquire the production side of Ferrari. The deal was made on a handshake. Soon, though, Ford's attorneys arrived in Italy with contracts, and an accounting crew arrived to take inventory. This was normal business procedure for the Americans, but Ferrari was insulted. After all, he had an understanding with a gentleman, not with a group of attorneys and accountants! The deal fell through.

One of the challenges for someone from a content culture is to realize the importance that context cultures place on building and maintaining personal relationships. That's certainly what a major in the U.S. Air Force discovered when he was on assignment in the Middle East: "The outgoing chief took his replacement to meet a key contact. I watched, stunned and helpless, as the new officer destroyed in five seconds what the incumbent had taken a year to build. Undoubtedly, the new chief thought he was creating the impact of a hard-charging young executive by barging into the contact's office and giving him a bone-crushing handshake, but in reality he was tearing down a delicate relationship."

Here's another way to look at this segment of cultural difference: It's well known that advanced industrialized nations rely heavily on technology and emphasize written communication over oral or face-to-face interactions. Certainly the United States, Canada, and northern Europe exemplify this trend. But Japan, which also has the latest technologies, still relies more on face-to-face communication. The determining factor may not be the degree of industrialization but rather whether the culture is one of context or content.

Affective versus Neutral Cultures

With much angry gesturing, an Italian manager referred to the idea of his Dutch counterpart as "crazy." The Dutch manager replied, "What do you mean 'crazy'? I've considered all the factors, and I think this is a viable approach. And calm down! We need to analyze this, not get sidetracked by emotional theatrics." At that point the Italian threw up his hands and walked out of the meeting.

In international business practices, reason and emotion both play a role. Which of these dominates depends on whether we are *affective* (readily showing emotions) or emotionally *neutral* in our approach. Members of neutral cultures do not telegraph their feelings but keep them carefully controlled and subdued. In cultures with high affect, people show their feelings plainly by laughing, smiling, grimacing, scowling, crying, shouting—or, sometimes, throwing up their hands and walking out of the room.

This doesn't mean that people in neutral cultures are cold or unfeeling. But in the course of normal business activities, people in neutral cultures are more careful to monitor the amount of emotion they display. Research conducted with people who were upset about something at work noted that only some cultures supported expressing those feelings openly. Emotional reactions were found to be *least* acceptable in Japan, Indonesia, the United Kingdom, Norway, and the Netherlands and *most* accepted in Italy, France, the United States, and Singapore.

There is a tendency for those from neutral cultures to dismiss anger, delight, or intensity in the workplace as unprofessional. And people from affective cultures may think of their passive colleagues as emotionally dead or as hiding their true feelings behind a mask of deceit. In reality, of course, there is nothing "good" or "bad" about these differences. They are just, well, different.

Nonverbal and Cross-cultural

Perception is at the heart of intercultural communication. We misperceive and misunderstand one another all the time, even when we share the same background. It just stands to reason that the process gets more complicated when we are communicating with those whose values and cultures are not the same as ours.

People around the world use body language to convey unspoken messages, but cultures develop specific rules about nonverbal etiquette. The most innocuous gestures—when misinterpreted—can wreak havoc on business dealings. The following are just a few basic examples of greeting behaviors, head nods, hand gestures, and eye contact cues that you might come across in a cross-cultural business meeting.

Greetings The greeting gesture that most businesspeople around the world use is the handshake, but even that has its cultural nuances. In the United States, the handshake is most often effusive. We use a strong grip and several pumps of the arm to deliver an unspoken message of confidence. A Brit may give three to five hand pumps; in Germany or France, one or two pumps is considered sufficient, with the pressure generally lighter. In Asia the grip is often rather limp. A light, lingering handshake is generally more favored in Latin America, and to withdraw the hand too quickly could be interpreted as an insult.

The nonverbal greeting you get depends on where you are.

Some cultures add a cheek kiss to the greeting. Scandinavians are happy with a single kiss, the French and the Spanish prefer a double, and the Dutch, Belgians, and Arabs go for a triple kiss. In Turkey, in addition to the normal handshake, a much younger person may kiss your hand and press it to his head as a sign of respect.

Exceptions to the handshake greeting can be seen in Japan and South Korea (bowing), in India (the *namaste*—palms held together in a prayer gesture), and in Arab and Islamic cultures (the salaam—touching the heart with the right palm and then sweeping the forearm up and outward).

TRY THIS

Take out your business card and exchange cards with a colleague. Now do the same thing but pretend you are in Asia. Do you know the difference?

In Asian business meetings you pass out business cards (using both hands, as you should to present any gift) to your counterparts in order of seniority. And, when handed a card by an Asian counterpart, you should study it before respectfully stowing it among your belongings. If you casually disregard the business cards of others—or bend, fold, or mutilate them—it is considered highly insulting.

Cards are presented and received with two hands in most Asian cultures.

Head nods—yes and no　A Canadian businesswoman, on a trip in India, stopped at the hotel's concierge desk to ask about transportation to her meeting. "Does the hotel have a car service you could recommend?" The man behind the counter shook his head from side to side. "Is there taxi service to the office building?" Again, the man shook his head. Frustrated, the woman asked, "Well, how can I get there?" The man behind the counter calmly answered, "Whichever way you prefer," while still moving his head from side to side.

In most parts of the world, shaking the head up and down indicates "yes" and shaking the head left to right indicates "no." Indians however, tend to shake their heads about 270 degrees to indicate a "yes" as well as a "no." This is a confusing gesture for people who do not understand the prevalence of this practice on the subcontinent.

The businesswoman might have been even more confused in Bulgaria, where a nod is "no" and a head shake means "yes." In Japan there's yet another twist: a nod of the head does not necessarily imply agreement; more often it only means that the listener has understood the message.

Eye contact　The rules of eye contact vary from culture to culture. The Finns and the French expect direct eye contact, whereas the Japanese and the South Koreans tend to avoid it, considering it impolite and intimidating. In the United States, direct eye contact between strangers lasts for only a split second. In Italy, Spain, and other Latin countries, there is prolonged eye contact. But in Latin America as well as some African cultures, prolonged eye contact from someone of lesser status is considered disrespectful. In the United States, people are taught to look at each other during conversations, but in some cultures avoiding eye contact by looking down is considered a sign of respect. Throughout Southeast Asia it's best to avoid prolonged eye contact until the relationship is firmly established.

Even the English and the Americans, whose nonverbal behavior is often aligned, have a problem seeing eye to eye. Researchers noted misunderstandings between English and American speakers because each was unsure whether the other comprehended what was being said. The problem was in their eye contact: the Englishman is taught to pay strict attention, to hold eye contact, and to listen carefully. He blinks his eyes to let you know he has heard you. Americans, on the other hand, are taught not to stare.

Hand signals   It's okay to talk with your hands if you know what they're saying. Gestures are powerful communicators in any culture and are obviously easier to learn than language. Just be aware that some very familiar hand gestures can have very different meanings.

To beckon someone in China, Korea, Taiwan, Japan, or the Philippines, place your hand palm down and move your fingers in a scratching motion. The gesture you see in North America (palm up with the index finger making a curling motion toward your body) is used only for animals.

The thumbs-up gesture that North Americans and many other cultures flash when they want to signify "Good job!" or "Well done!" is considered offensive in certain locales, Australia and Nigeria to mention just two. When you order drinks in Germany, the gesture means "One, please."

When someone taps the side of his nose with his forefinger, in many cultures it signals a desire for confidentiality or secrecy. But in the United Kingdom, Holland, and Austria, if the tap is to the front of the nose, it means "Mind your own business."

Flashing the V-sign for victory in the United States suggests that business negotiations have concluded well. But if the back of the hand is facing out, that sentiment will be lost on anyone from the United Kingdom, Australia, and New Zealand and is interpreted as a rude gesture.

The crossed-fingers gesture (the American "Good luck!" signal—or the cancellation sign when telling a lie) has several other meanings. In Turkey the gesture is used to break a friendship. Elsewhere it is used to indicate that something is good or to swear an oath—and as a symbol for copulation.

The eyelid pull, in which the forefinger is placed on the cheekbone and pulled down to widen the eye a little, translates to "I am alert" in France, Germany, Yugoslavia, and Turkey. In Spain and Italy, it means "Be alert." In Austria it signals boredom. In Saudi Arabia touching the lower eyelid with the forefinger indicates stupidity.

Even the "okay" sign commonly used in the United States as signifying approval is a gesture that has several different meanings according to the country. In France it means zero, in Japan it is a symbol for money, and in Brazil it carries a vulgar connotation.

As globalization remains a major factor in business, organizations and customers from a host of different cultures are insisting that we become sensitive to their ways. Professionals who try to negotiate or sell or even interact without that sensitivity will undoubtedly lose business opportunities.

It's a fact of life. People from any culture prefer to do business with those who put them at ease. Although you can't learn every gesture and facial expression used around the world, you can develop a curiosity about, and a deep respect for, the multitude of differences. It's just good manners—and good business!

CHAPTER 10

Selling Your Message without Saying a Word

I WAS TOLD THAT PAUL, the senior manager I had been asked to coach, was a poor communicator. After watching him at a leadership conference, I was in total agreement. It wasn't what Paul said. His words were carefully chosen and well rehearsed. It was his nonverbal language. Mechanical in all his gestures, Paul's body was screaming: "I'm uncomfortable and unconvinced about everything I'm telling you!"

Then there was the matter of timing. If a person's gestures are produced before or as the words come out, he appears open and candid. If he speaks first and then gestures, however, as Paul did, it's perceived as a contrived movement. And at that point, the validity of whatever is said comes under suspicion.

The question: Could I help?

The answer: Not much.

Oh sure, I could find ways to make Paul's movements less wooden and his timing more fluid, but what he really needed was genuine passion!

I've learned a lot of things as a therapist, speaker, and coach. Most of all I've learned that the foundation of effective body language has to be honesty. If you don't believe the message you're delivering, if you don't genuinely care about the people you're trying to motivate or serve, or if you personally wouldn't buy the product or service you are selling, at some point your body cues will leak the truth.

I wanted to tell you that story before going into this final chapter in which you'll learn how to make your body language more positive and powerful. If you are trying to fool people into thinking you are sincere when you're not, you'll need a lot more than a few nonverbal tricks. But if you want to project your most authentic self—and use effective body language to help you do so—this chapter is full of the tips and techniques that will help you do just that! You'll learn how to make a positive first impression in a matter of seconds. You'll discover what body language signals to use to build strong relationships with clients and customers and co-workers. You'll get tips on how to project confidence when making a business presentation.

It all starts with knowing how other people are translating your nonverbal messages.

Your Body Language as Others Read It

To change your body language, you must first be aware of what your body is saying. And this isn't as easy as you may think. Take Sara, for example.

A vice president at a utility company, Sara complained that she was consistently overlooked for senior positions. "I don't know what I'm doing wrong," she told me. "I'm smart, enthusiastic, and hardworking. I can't figure out why people don't warm up to me."

Well, maybe *she* couldn't figure it out, but if you saw her in action, you'd know exactly what her problem was.

During my session with Sara, her eyes darted around the room as if searching for the nearest exit, her hands made choppy gestures, and she drummed her fingers on the conference table. I'd been with the woman for only an hour and already I was just as jumpy as she made all her business colleagues feel when dealing with her.

Sara perceived herself as projecting enthusiasm and energy, but the nonverbal cues she displayed were picked up as impatience and nervousness.

This is a common situation with body language. Often your nonverbal signals don't convey what you intended them to. You may be slouching because you're tired, but people read it as disinterest. You may be more comfortable standing with your arms folded across your chest (or you may be cold), but others see you as resistant and unapproachable. And keeping your hands stiffly by your side or stuck in your pockets can give the impression that you're insecure—whether you are or not.

With nonverbal communication it's not how the sender feels that matters most; it is how the observer *perceives* how the sender feels. And those interpretations are often made deep in the subconscious mind, based on a primitive emotional reaction that hasn't changed much since humans first began interacting with one another.

TRY THIS

When preparing for your next job interview, important meeting, or big presentation, rehearse in front of a video camera. Then view the video, staying as objective as possible. If you can hire a coach to help you, that's even better. But if you will just keep in mind what you've learned in this book, you can successfully critique your own performance.

Just remember to be kind to yourself. Clients are often stunned by their body language when they watch themselves for the first time. After viewing his recording of a mock job interview, an incredulous client exclaimed, "Hell, I wouldn't hire me!"

*"May I offer a bit of constructive criticism?
When you're having lunch with a client, don't carve
little dollar signs in your mashed potatoes."*

Seven Seconds to Make a Positive First Impression

You're at a conference and you turn to the stranger standing next to you. He turns to face you, and in that instant your brain makes a thousand computations. Is he someone to approach or to avoid? Should you flee or be friendly? Will he harm you or help you? After about seven seconds, you've already decided whether you like him. Sure, your opinion may change once you get to know the man better, but that first impression will always linger.

And, by the way, while you're consciously and unconsciously evaluating him, he's also making the same kind of instantaneous judgments about you.

In business first impressions are crucial. Once someone mentally labels you as likable or unlikable, everything else you do will be viewed through that filter. If someone likes you, she'll look for the best in you. If she doesn't like you or mistrusts you, she'll suspect devious motives in all your actions.

Although you can't stop people from making snap decisions—the human brain is hardwired in this way as a prehistoric survival mechanism—you *can* understand how to make those decisions work in your favor.

First impressions are more heavily influenced by nonverbal cues than by verbal cues. In fact, studies have found that nonverbal cues have more than four times the impact on the impression you make than anything you say. Luckily, the same nonverbal factors that draw you to certain people are what others are instinctively looking for in you.

We all want to interact and do business with people who are trustworthy and energizing, who put us at ease and make us feel good about ourselves. Luckily, these are the very qualities that you can project nonverbally in those first crucial seven seconds. Every encounter, from conferences to meetings to training sessions to business lunches, presents an opportunity to meet people, network, and expand your professional contacts by "managing your impression."

Here are six powerful ways to make a positive first impression.

1. Adjust your attitude People pick up your attitude instantly. Before you turn to greet someone, enter an office for a business interview, or step on-stage to make a presentation, think about the situation and make a conscious choice about the attitude you want to embody. Attitudes that attract people include curious, friendly, happy, receptive, patient, approachable, welcoming, and helpful. Attitudes that are off-putting include angry, impatient, bored, arrogant, fearful, disheartened, and suspicious.

2. Smile A smile is an invitation, a sign of welcome. It says, "I'm friendly and approachable."

3. Make eye contact Looking at someone's eyes transmits energy and indicates interest and openness. To improve your eye contact, make a practice of noticing the eye color of everyone you meet.

4. Raise your eyebrows Open your eyes slightly more than normal to simulate the eyebrow flash that is the nonverbal signal of recognition and acknowledgment.

5. Shake hands This is the quickest way to establish rapport. It's also the most effective. Research shows that it takes an average of three hours of continuous interaction to develop the same level of rapport that you can get with a single handshake.

6. Lean in slightly Leaning forward shows that you're engaged and interested. But be respectful of the other person's space. That means, in most business situations, staying about two feet away.

TRY THIS

Once you've passed the seven-second test and are engaged in conversation with another person, you can create a lasting and positive impact by adding a single nonverbal component to a simple verbal statement. Here's how to do it: When you meet someone and she tells you her name, find a way to repeat that name later in the conversation. And as you do, anchor the positive emotion (which your use of their name evokes) by touching the person lightly on the forearm.

The impact of this brief touch comes from the fact that you have aroused positive feelings in an individual by remembering and using her name, and as you touch her arm, those positive emotions get linked (or anchored) to your touch. Then at subsequent meetings you can reactivate that initial favorable impression by once again lightly touching your acquaintance's arm.

Body Language through the Eyes of Your Customers

We've all experienced lousy customer service and the non-verbal signals that often accompany it. It's the salesperson who's on the phone— obviously on a personal call—and who continues the conversation while turning her back on you. It's the receptionist who greets you with a disinterested and bored expression. It's the human resource manager who rolls his eyes and sighs at your request for more information. Unfortunately, it's an experience that happens all too often to all of us!

But this meant nothing to Ralph, a no-nonsense kind of businessman who had built his reputation and career on getting things done. Although he frequently gave presentations to key clients, Ralph had relied solely on his professional competence to win them over. Why should he be concerned about body language and customer relationships?

It was a good question, and I had to think for a bit before coming up with the following example.

Of all the professions that should be totally focused on the quality of the work done, the medical profession would rate high on most people's lists. (Nobody wants an incompetent doctor!) And yet research on why patients sue doctors reveals that basic interpersonal skills (what is now referred to as *clinical empathy*) can be just as important as clinical skills in preventing lawsuits.

The most successful doctor/patient relationships are personal.

The most important factor in many potential legal cases, besides the injury itself, is the quality of the doctor/patient relationship. And a big part of that relationship depends on nonverbal communication. One study found that greater than 50 percent of 263 patients who sued their doctor claimed they were so turned off by the doctor that they wanted to sue him or her before the alleged event occurred!

The Ralph I referred to earlier was not a doctor. But if you are like Ralph and think that relationships with customers really don't matter in *your* business, I'd ask you to reconsider. I don't know of any profession—from healthcare to high tech—where customer relationships and body language are *not* a crucial part of business success.

Regardless of the industry you work in, there are some basic principles that apply to any profession. Look at the following research findings about the doctor/patient relationship and notice the similarities in your own line of work.

- Patients report greater satisfaction when doctors show nonverbal indicators of interest—such as leaning forward, nodding and gesturing more, establishing closer interpersonal distance, and spending less time looking at charts.

- A crucial point in the doctor/patient encounter is the physician's first greeting. Does the physician show personal concern by offering a handshake, maintaining eye contact, and giving a warm smile?

- Patients think they have spent more time with a doctor who sits down versus one who remains standing. That's because a sitting position communicates interest and attentiveness to what the patient is saying, whereas a standing position may give the impression of control and an authoritative attitude.

- Doctors who look at their watches, drum their fingers, and look toward the door give the impression that they're in a hurry or don't have time for the patient.

- If a doctor shies away from the patient, doesn't lean toward the patient, or seems uncomfortable in the session, the body language communicates a problem that is sometimes not even stated.

- Poor body language in emotionally charged situations can lead to a breakdown in the doctor/patient relationship.

It's also interesting to note that doctors who are competent with nonverbal communication have higher patient satisfaction scores. They are rated as more caring. And, whether you are a physician, salesperson, teacher, coach, negotiator, team leader, or senior manager, *caring* is a key component in your professional relationships. To quote Mark Twain, "People don't care how much you know until they know how much you care."

Who's your customer? You may be in retail, where your customer walks into your shop. Or you may work in a large enterprise, where your customer is someone in another part of the organization. But wherever you are, it's highly likely that part of your job involves customer satisfaction. And a big part of satisfying customers is the body language you use when dealing with them.

TRY THIS

Think about what it's like to be an internal or external customer of yours. How would you rate your personal level of service, courtesy, and respect? (You can also ask your customers to rate your service level.) Then think about the role that nonverbal signals play in how you are perceived. If you are sending mixed messages (for instance, saying, "I'd be delighted to help you" while your gestures and expression signal the opposite), all that wonderful verbiage means nothing. Customers believe that what your body says is the *real* message.

Body Language On-stage

Whether you are speaking to a business audience of five hundred, pitching a product/service to potential buyers, or presenting your idea at a team meeting, you are "on-stage." And whenever you are on-stage, nonverbal signals are key. People will be judging you by your appearance and your body language. And they'll do it quickly. Often the audience will have come to a conclusion about you and your presentation before you've even had a chance to dazzle them with *any* of your content.

"Before I begin, let me apologize for my appearance; apparently there's a full moon this evening."

I don't mean that your words don't matter. Obviously, if you want people to be convinced, emotionally touched, or motivated to action, you will need to have relevant and meaningful content when you address them. But because body language sets up the initial perception, you'll also need the following do's and don'ts to gain the *non*verbal advantage.

- **Do** get out and let the audience see your whole body.

- **Don't** hide behind the lectern.

- **Do** stand centered on both feet (about shoulder width apart) with your knees slightly bent.

- **Don't** rock backward and forward or shift your weight from foot to foot. You will appear distracted or unsure of yourself.

- **Do** open your body. Keep your shoulders back and your upper body relaxed. Always show your hands and use open-palm gestures.

- **Don't** keep your arms too close to your body. Hands clasped behind your back make you look like you're being arrested; hands clasped in front (the protective "fig leaf" position) make you look unsure of yourself.

- **Do** take your time making eye contact. Look at individuals in the audience for at least three to five seconds to really connect.

- **Don't** let your gaze sweep the audience too quickly or get stuck addressing only one part of the room.

- **Do** move around. Human beings are drawn to movement. Our brains are programmed to pay attention to it.

- **Don't** move constantly, however. You are most effective when you combine movement with physical pauses in which you stand absolutely still and highlight some key points.

TRY THIS

The next time you are preparing to give a presentation to any size audience, begin by defining your goal. For example, you might be trying to close a sale, get your boss to consider you for a promotion, or motivate your organization to embrace change. Whatever your objective is, use that as your framework for choosing supportive body language.

If you want to project authority and control, disregard some of the rules you've just learned. Control and authority can be underscored by standing behind the lectern, minimizing your gestures, and making limited eye contact. But if projecting sincerity, caring, or concern is part of your message, you'll get better results by keeping in mind the guidelines I've stated.

The Silent Language of Leadership

Managers looking to help their organizations, their teams, or their departments thrive in the twenty-first century need to forget about issuing orders or coercing with threats. Success in today's world takes employee engagement and creative collaboration—both of which must be freely given. You can't force people to care or create or share their best ideas with others, but you can influence their behavior and motivate them to achieve great things.

To be a successful leader at any level of the organization, you need to tune in to the body language of those you lead so that you can understand the meaning behind what's being said. That's why all the nonverbal cues you've learned in this book will be extremely valuable. But you also need to be aware that nonverbally you are constantly expressing your feelings, your likes and dislikes, and your expectations. (All leaders express enthusiasm, warmth, and confidence—as well as arrogance, indifference, and displeasure through their facial expressions, gestures, touch, and use of space.)

When your nonverbal messages conflict with your verbal messages, the people you are talking to become confused. Mixed signals have a negative effect on performance and make it almost impossible to build relationships of trust. This is true whether you are the chief executive officer, a department head, a team leader, or a first-line supervisor.

Consider, for example, the oil company CEO who showed up at a refinery in an expensive suit and tie to discuss the firm's state of affairs with rank-and-file operators, electricians, and members of the warehouse staff, who were dressed in their blue, fire-retardant overalls. That was just the beginning. After being introduced and walking to the front of the room, he removed his wristwatch (probably a Rolex) and quite visibly placed it on the lectern. The unspoken message: "I'm a very busy man, you can tell I don't like coming into dirty places like this, and I have exactly twenty minutes to spend with you." That message was quite different from the words he actually used to begin his comments: "I'm happy to be with you today."

Which message do you think those refinery workers believed—the CEO's spoken words or what his body language said?

The Body Language of Inclusion

No leader, regardless of how intelligent he or she may be, can succeed alone. Leaders need the support, energy, and ideas of others. In my research over the past twenty-five years, I've found that great leaders are great collaborators, able to make everyone feel like they are *all* part of the team. People work for bosses, but they work *with* leaders.

A great leader is one of the team.

TRY THIS

At your next face-to-face meeting with a team member or colleague, remember that building inclusion has everything to do with your body language. If you incorporate the following positive nonverbal messages into your conversation, you will be sending signals of trust and respect.

▶ Face people directly (heart to heart). Even a quarter-turn away signals a lack of interest and makes the speaker shut down.

▶ Remove barriers between you and the other person. Take away things that block your view. Move the phone or stacks of paper on your desk. Better still, come out from behind your desk.

▶ Maintain positive eye contact. Remember that people will assume you are not listening (and not interested) if your eyes scan the room or if your gaze shifts to paperwork or your computer screen.

▶ Use palm-up hand gestures when speaking. They send messages of candor and openness.

▶ Synchronize your body language with the person you are dealing with. Subtly match their stance, arm positions, and facial expressions.

▶ Use head nods. This signal encourages people to continue speaking and signals that you appreciate their comments.

The Body Language of Motivation

Pygmalion in the Classroom, one of the most controversial publications in the history of educational research, shows how a teacher's expectations can motivate student achievement. This classic study gave prospective teachers a list of students who had been identified as high achievers. The teachers were told to expect remarkable results from these students, and at the end of the year the students did indeed make sharp increases on their IQ test scores.

In reality, these children had been chosen at random, not as a result of any testing. It was the teachers' belief in their potential that was responsible for the extraordinary results. The children were never told they were high achievers, but this message was delivered subtly and nonverbally through expectancy behaviors such as facial expressions, gestures, touch, and spatial relationships.

TRY THIS

Imagine that you found out that everyone on your staff had been identified as a high achiever. And imagine that this was a secret you couldn't share with anyone on your staff—except through your body language. What nonverbal signals would you use to let people know they were special? More eye contact? Appreciative nods? Smiles?

Once you get a good idea of what you would do, take one full week and nonverbally treat everyone who works for or with you as if they were potential stars. See if at least some of them don't start living up to the high expectations your body language signals send.

Dress for Success

My friend Joyce is an educator and an entrepreneur. One of the secrets of her success is the way she dresses. Even when traveling for a vacation, Joyce is in a business suit and heels. Her motto: "Wear great clothes. You never know whom you'll meet!"

She may be onto something.

You can't *not* communicate. Everything you do makes some kind of statement. The fact that Joyce wears a business suit and not jeans and a T-shirt sends a message.

The old saying "You can't judge a book by its cover" may be true, but book-jacket and product-packaging designers around the world have built an industry betting that people *do* judge—and purchase—products based on how they look. And career counselors still advise clients to dress for the job they *want,* not the job they currently have. Counselors know that people are judged, at least to some degree, by their appearance—and they want their clients to gain a nonverbal advantage by already looking the part.

Which brings me back to you and your "personal packaging." Office-appropriate attire has certainly changed over the years. Formal business suits aren't a requirement in many workplaces, and the options available often lead to some questionable choices. As one management consultant told me: "In today's world of business casual, it sometimes does seem

"Didn't anyone tell you about casual Fridays?"

like anything goes. To be fair, most of my clients' employees display common sense when making their fashion statements, but I've also seen some less-than-subtle expressions of taste (or lack thereof), even in critical engagements."

Clothes make a strong visual statement about how you see yourself. Comfort may aid productivity but, in this era of "Me, Inc." and "the Brand Called You," are flip-flops, sweats, jeans, and flashy or revealing clothing part of how you want to be judged? You might think you are expressing your individuality, but you could also be sending the message that you're not a serious professional.

Clothing has an effect on both the wearer and the observer. It has been proven that people are more likely to give money (tips, charitable donations, and the like) or information to someone if that person is well dressed.

TRY THIS

Experiment with your appearance. Notice how people react to you when you wear certain colors or styles. Then, based on those reactions and your career goals, you can make an informed decision about how you want to "package" yourself.

Appropriate dress is a way of expressing respect for the situation and the people in it, so your look may change depending on the business circumstances.

Teresa is a management consultant—and a master at dressing for the role. She loves to wear hot pink, turquoise, and fire-engine red silk dresses with stiletto heels and lots of bling to work in her New York City office. But the moment she has to meet with a conservative client or one who is going through difficult times, Teresa transforms herself into a prim professional whose outfit matches the way she wants to be perceived. (In her words, "The success I dress for is that of my *client*.") One member of her staff recalls meeting Teresa at

What message do you want to send?

the headquarters of a nonprofit religious organization, where they were to conduct focus groups. The staff member barely recognized her stylish boss. By dressing more like the client, Teresa fit right in. She looked like one of the nuns!

The Body Language of Charisma

Max Weber, the father of sociology, first coined the term *charisma* to describe inspirational leaders. Originally from the Greek *kharisma,* meaning favor or divine gift, charisma has also been defined as "part confidence, part presence, and part sex appeal." But however we define it, we know it when we see it. We call someone charismatic when they somehow compel us to embrace their vision—whether it's corporate, social, religious, or political.

In the context of this chapter, I define charisma as body language that is completely congruent with the spoken word. Whether you are in management, sales, customer service, healthcare, or education, you are the most charismatic and convincing when what you are feeling internally is perfectly aligned with what you're expressing.

I'm not the only expert to notice the connection between body language and charisma. Howard Friedman, a psychology professor at the University of California at Riverside, measures charisma by studying such nonverbal cues as facial expressions, gestures, and body movements. He finds that charismatic people smile naturally (with wrinkling around the eyes), use a variety of gestures, and touch others during conversations. Friedman has developed what he calls the Affective Communication Test, which some large U.S. corporations use to measure the charisma of potential leaders. And it seems to be valid. Toyota's top U.S. salesman scored in the ninety-fifth percentile, and the sales manager of a leading hair replacement company scored in the ninety-ninth.

You Are "a Natural"

I once worked with the head of a research department who was preparing for a major presentation. One-on-one, this man was smart and charming and had a great sense of humor. His body language was congruent and expressive. But he was also an introvert. Put him on-stage in front of an audience and he became a nonverbal disaster. He didn't need to work on technique so much as he needed to relax and let his natural personality and body language speak.

You may be in a similar situation. When talking with friends, you use your hands and face to help describe an event or object. You smile, frown, shrug your shoulders, and make broad sweeping gestures. Just remember that your business audience also relies on your nonverbal communication to understand the bigger, more inspiring picture.

Sometimes all you have to do to be truly impressive is to get out of your own way!

Standing Tall

In the U.S. population, about 14.5 percent of all men are 6 feet tall or taller. Among CEOs of Fortune 500 companies, that number is 58 percent. Even more strikingly, in the general American population 3.9 percent of adult men are 6 feet 2 inches or taller. Among the CEOs 30 percent are 6 feet 2 inches or taller. Somewhere in the American psyche, we have equated height with leadership ability.

"I read someplace that tall employees get better pay and faster promotions."

Although it is unlikely that you will grow another 4 or 5 inches, you can appear taller and more authoritative by holding your body erect. Especially in formal speaking situations, how you stand is vital. Standing tall with an upright posture and your head held high is the body language of competence, confidence, and power.

The Body/Mind Connection

You already know that the way you feel affects your body language. If you are depressed, you tend to round your shoulders, slump, and look down. If you are upbeat, you tend to smile and hold yourself erect. But did you know that the reverse is also true? Your gestures, your movements, the way you hold and carry yourself, and even your facial expressions affect your emotions by sending messages back to your brain.

In several experiments individuals were asked to smile and were then shown pictures of various events. The smiling participants reported that the pictures pleased them and even made them feel elated. When asked to frown during the same kind of experiment, subjects reported feelings of annoyance and anger. Additional studies demonstrated not only that a smile is a consequence of feeling happy or content but also that putting on a smile can induce physiological changes in body temperature, heart rate, and skin resistance.

The best way to create a smile is to think of something or someone that genuinely amuses or delights you. But consider research findings that found that even if the smile were mechanically produced, positive feelings still emerged. This study had matched samples of people looking at Gary Larson cartoons. The first group ranked every cartoon as funnier than did the second group. The only difference is that members of the first group were asked to hold a pencil crosswise between their back teeth. The simulated smile caused by the pencil between their teeth affected their emotion—and their perception of the cartoons as funnier.

TRY THIS

Let's face it, confidence counts. A lot. I've seen many qualified people get passed over for promotion, lose a sale, or fail an interview simply because they couldn't project a confident attitude.

The next time you go into a situation in which you want to project your most confident self, you can start by standing up straight, pulling your shoulders back, and holding your head high. Just by assuming this physical position, you will begin to feel surer of yourself. And if you add a genuine smile (or even a pencil between your teeth), you will affect your brain and emotions even more positively!

Putting It All Together

So you're ready for your close-up—or at least an important presentation, a talk to a professional group, a job interview, or maybe just looking ahead to your day-to-day interactions with partners, peers, managers, team members, customers, and the people who report to you.

It's likely, if it *is* some special presentation, that you've chosen just the right words, prepared just the right visuals, maybe even rehearsed what you are going to say. By now you've also gained some insight into all the nonverbal signals that are a key part of the message you're sending—and why it's so important to understand what your body is *really* communicating.

Know what their   **Don't know what their**
bodies are saying   **bodies are saying**

So there you have it—everything I've learned about nonverbal communication in the past twenty-five years as a therapist, coach, professional speaker, and seminar presenter. But I'm still leaning, still researching, and still making new discoveries. And everything I learn in the future (along with articles and other resources on this topic) will be posted to www.NonverbalAdvantage.com. I hope you will visit me there to learn more, ask questions, and share your success stories. I'm looking forward to hearing from you!

Acknowledgments

I'd like to acknowledge the contribution of Dave Orman, whose critique and insights I relied on while writing this book.

I value and appreciate the immeasurable support of Brad Whitworth, who knows *all* the right people.

I'm beholden (once again) to Bob Dilenschneider for his unwavering encouragement.

I'm grateful to Pat Welch of Chameleon Design for his artistic contributions.

I'm indebted to Mark Andersen, Donna Barstow, Randy Glasbergen, Jonny VanOrman, and Signe Wilkinson for the use of their wonderful cartoons.

And, finally, I'd like to thank the entire team at Berrett-Koehler for their creativity, passion, and guidance.

Index

About the Author

Carol Kinsey Goman, PhD, is the president of Kinsey Consulting Services in Berkeley, California. As a consultant, Carol helps organizations thrive in an environment of ongoing, accelerating change. As a coach, she helps executives and managers become more effective communicators.

Carol presents keynote addresses and seminars for corporate clients, government agencies, and major trade associations around the world. Recent keynote speeches include:

- "The Nonverbal Advantage"

- "The Silent Language of Leadership"

- "Managing People through Continuous Change"

- "Thriving on Change"

- "Collaboration Is a Leadership Skill"

In addition to *The Nonverbal Advantage,* Carol has authored nine business books, including *"This Isn't the Company I Joined": How to Lead in a Business Turned Upside Down* and *Ghost Story,* a business fable about the power of collaboration.

Carol has been cited as an authority in media such as *Industry Week, Investor's Business Daily,* CNN's *Business Unusual, Bloomberg TV,* and the *NBC Nightly News.* She has served as adjunct faculty at John F. Kennedy University in the international MBA program, at the University of California in the Executive Education Department, and for the Chamber of Commerce of the United States at its Institutes for Organization Management.

You can contact Carol by e-mail at CGoman@CKG.com, by telephone at (510) 526-1727, or through her Web sites: www.CKG.com and www.NonverbalAdvantage.com.